I0469776

# Waterloo Ontario Book 1 in Colour Photos, Saving Our History One Photo at a Time

Photography
by Barbara Raué
updated 2016

Series Name:
Cruising Ontario

Book 114: Waterloo Book 1

Cover photo: 36 Young Street, Page 19

# Series Name: Cruising Ontario
## Saving Our History One Photo at a Time
### in colour photos

# Other Books by Barbara Raue

Coins of Gold

Arrows, Indians and Love

The Life and Times of Barbara
Volume 1: Inventions That Have Enhanced My Life
Volume 2: Entertainment That I Have Enjoyed
Volume 3: East Coast Trips
Volume 4: Olympics Have Always Intrigued Me
Volume 5: Wonders of the World
Volume 6: Caribbean Cruises We Have Enjoyed
Volume 7: Animals
Volume 8: Storms and Other Major Disasters in My Lifetime
Volume 9: Wars, Terrorist Attacks and Major Disasters

The Cromwell Family Book

Laura Secord Discovered

Visit Barbara's website to view all of her books
http://barbararaue.ca

Waterloo is a city in Southern Ontario. The Conestogo Parkway and Highway 8 connect Waterloo with Kitchener, Cambridge, Highway 7/8, and Highway 401. Waterloo shares several of its north-south arterial roads with neighboring Kitchener.

Waterloo was built on land that was part of a parcel of 675,000 acres assigned in 1784 to the Iroquois alliance that made up the League of Six Nations. Almost immediately, the native groups began to sell some of the land. Between 1796 and 1798, 93,000 acres were sold through a Crown Grant to Richard Beasley, with the Six Nations Indians continuing to hold the mortgage on the lands.

The first immigrants to the area were Mennonites from Pennsylvania. They bought deeds to land parcels from Beasley and began moving into the area in 1804. The following year, a group of twenty-six Mennonites pooled resources to purchase all of the unsold land from Beasley and discharge the mortgage held by the Six Nations Indians.

The Mennonites divided the land into smaller lots; two lots initially owned by Abraham Erb became the central core of Waterloo. Erb built a sawmill on Beaver, now Laurel, Creek in 1808 and in 1816 built the area's first grist mill which farmers from miles around used to grind their wheat into flour, a very important staple.

In 1816, the new township was named after Waterloo, Belgium, the site of the Battle of Waterloo, which had ended the Napoleonic Wars in Europe. After that war, the area became a popular destination for German immigrants. By the 1840s, German settlers were the dominant segment of the population. Many Germans settled in the small hamlet to the southeast of Waterloo. In their honour, the village was named Berlin in 1833 (renamed to Kitchener in 1916). Berlin was chosen as the site of the seat for the County of Waterloo in 1853.

The inhabitants established Waterloo as an important industrial and commercial centre. The village had a council chamber, fire hall, post office, library, and four steam-powered factories, including the Granite Mills and Distillery which became the Seagram Company.

The Grand River flows southward along the east side of the city. Its most significant tributary within the city is Laurel Creek, whose source lies just to the west of the city limits and its mouth just to the east, and crosses much of the city's central areas including the University of Waterloo lands and Waterloo Park; it flows under the uptown area in a culvert. In the west end of the city, the Waterloo Moraine provides over 300,000 people in the region with drinking water. Much of the gently hilly Waterloo Moraine underlies existing developed areas.

The main campuses of the University of Waterloo and Wilfrid Laurier University are located in Waterloo.

These municipalities surround Waterloo: Wellesley, St. Jacobs, Elmira, Conestogo and West Montrose, Guelph, Cambridge, Kitchener, Stratford, Wilmot and St. Agatha.

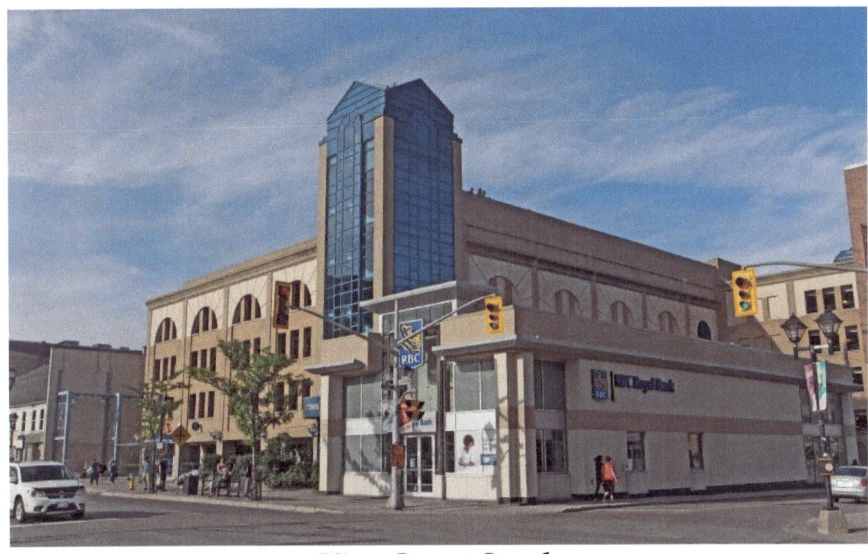

King Street South

# Table of Contents

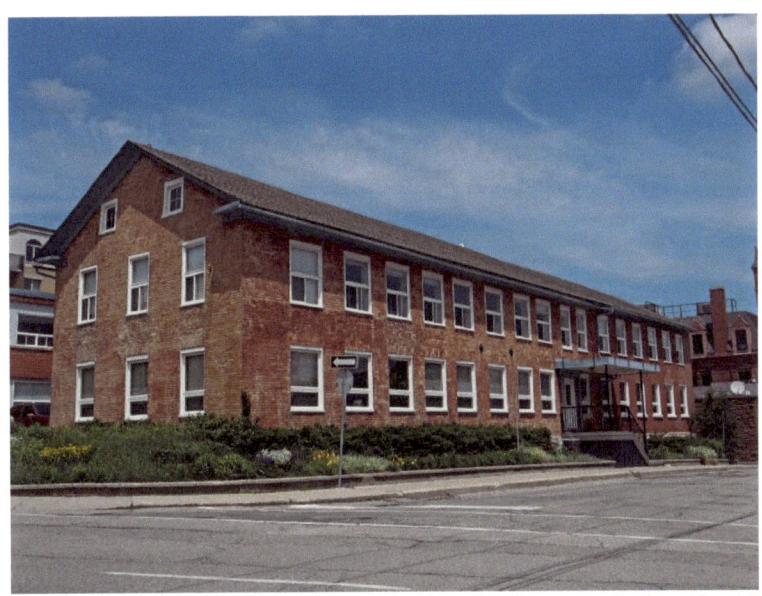

12 Dupont Street West – Albert Hotel built c. 1860; expanded as the Market Hotel c. 1874 – Georgian-Mennonite style - catered to farmers and commercial travellers visiting the Waterloo market.  Beginning in 1917, the John Forsyth Company converted it to a pajama and underwear factory; Forsyth products were widely acclaimed for their quality and custom fit.

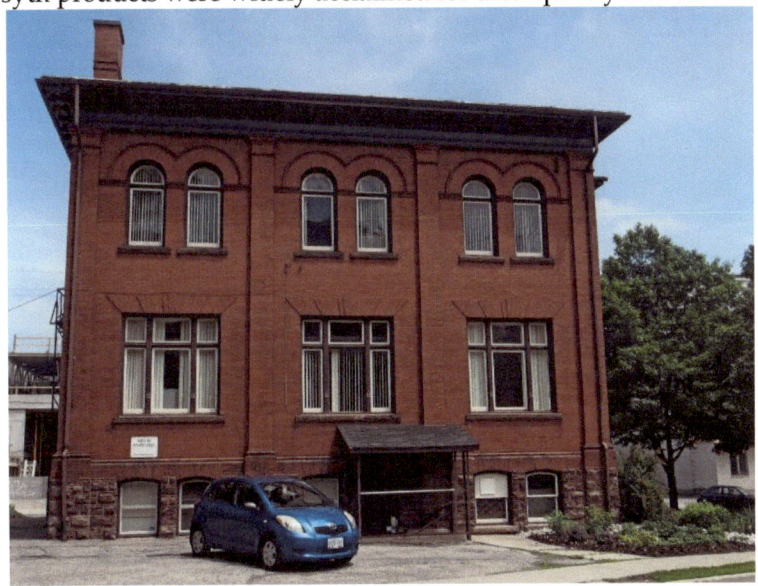

40 Albert Street

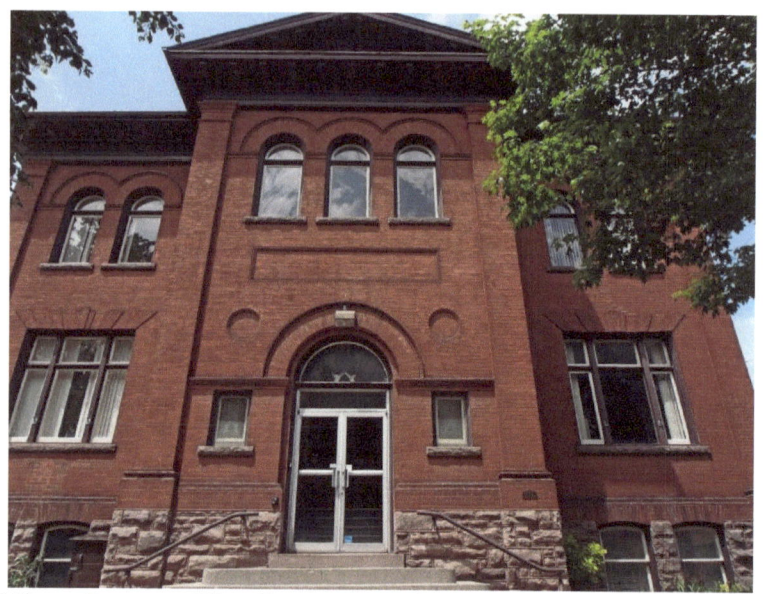

40 Albert Street – The Carnegie Library 1903 – rough ashlar sandstone from the Credit River valley as a foundation, and red pressed-bricks from Milton – Classical Revival style – semi-circular arch over entrance and second-storey windows, deep overhang of the eaves, triangular pediment, pilasters

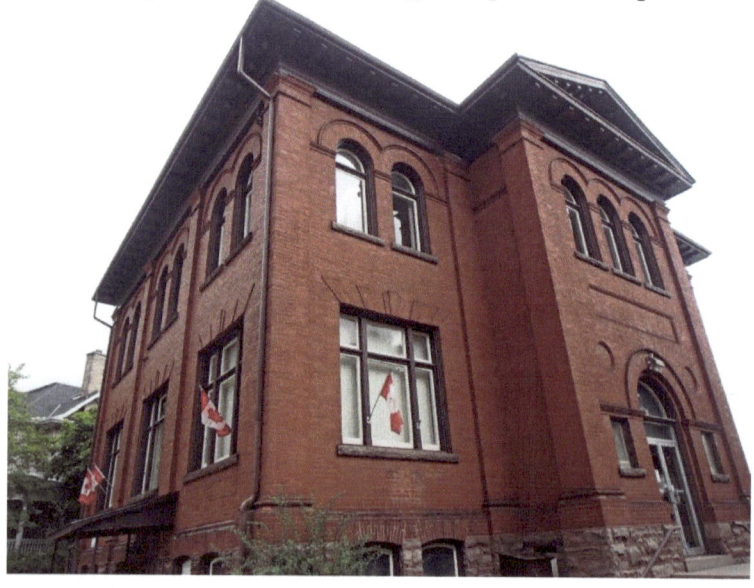

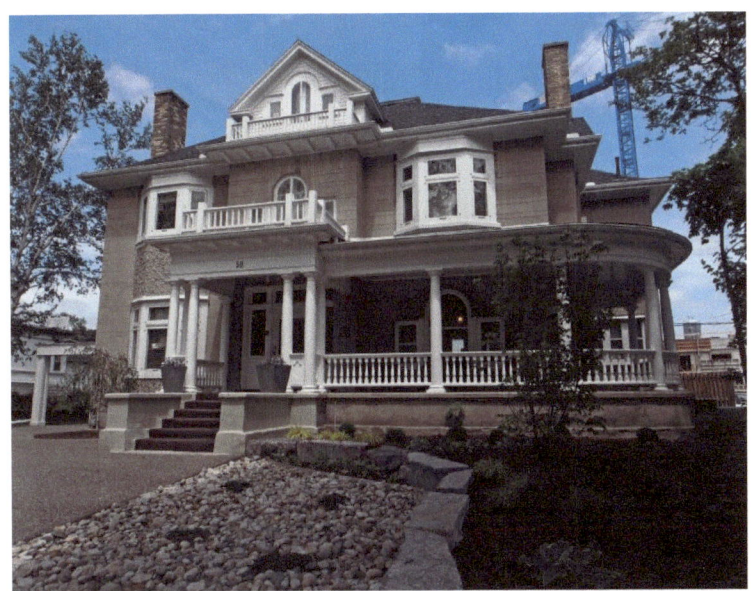

50 Albert Street – 1903 – Snyder-Seagram House – Edwardian Classical in parged concrete – superposed sets of Palladian windows and bay windows projecting over both storeys; curved, wraparound verandah with classical columns

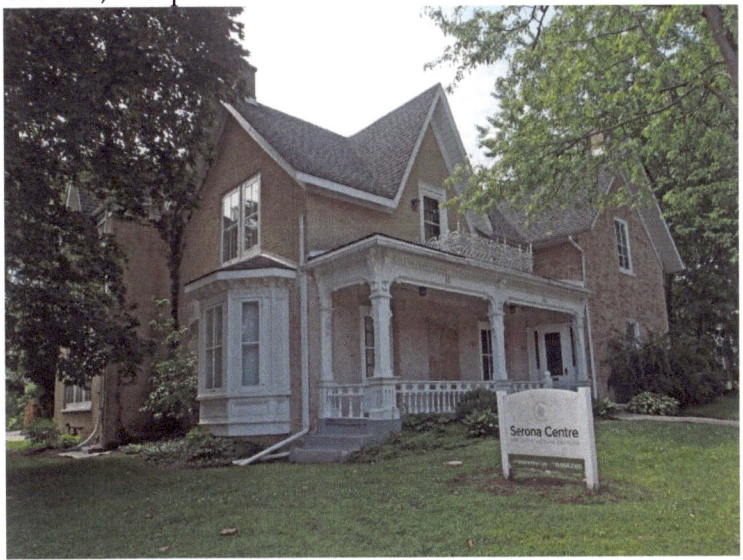

49 Albert Street – buff brick Gothic Revival, six-over-six paned windows, local yellow brick, iron railing on porch roof

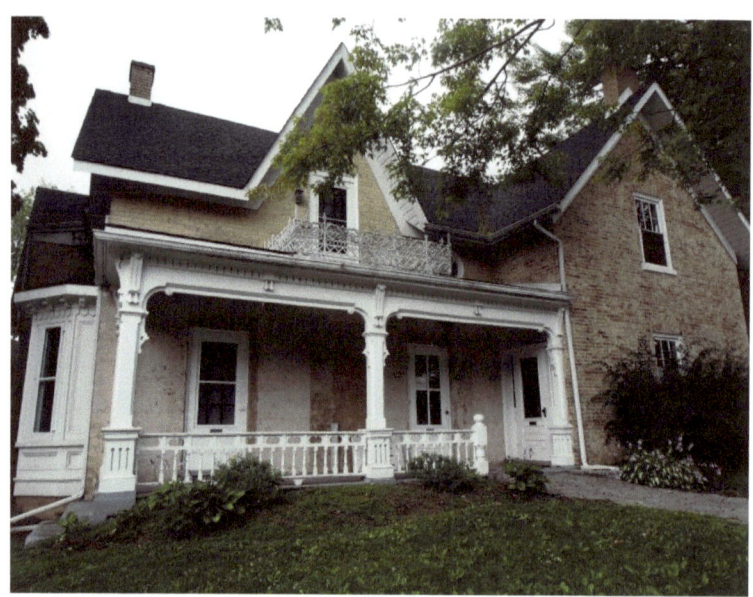

49 Albert Street – buff brick Gothic Revival house built in 1855 for George Randall and William Hespeler who ran the Granite Mill before it was sold to Joseph Seagram and became Seagram's Distillery.

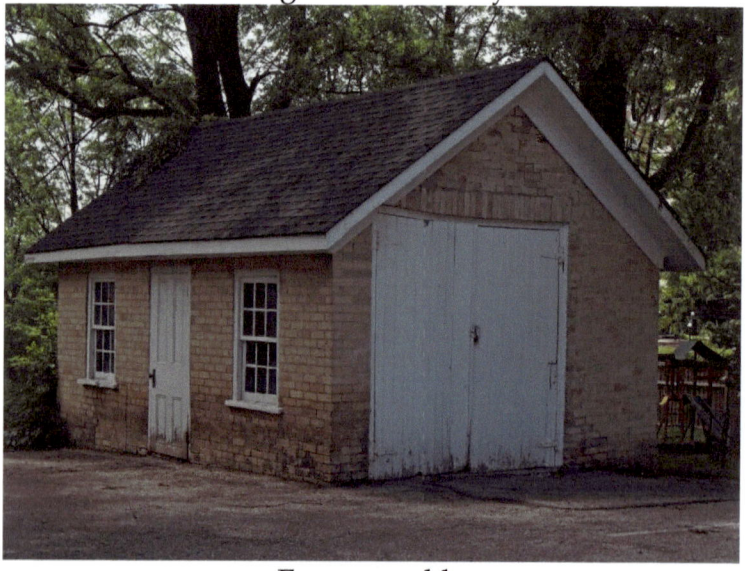

Former stable

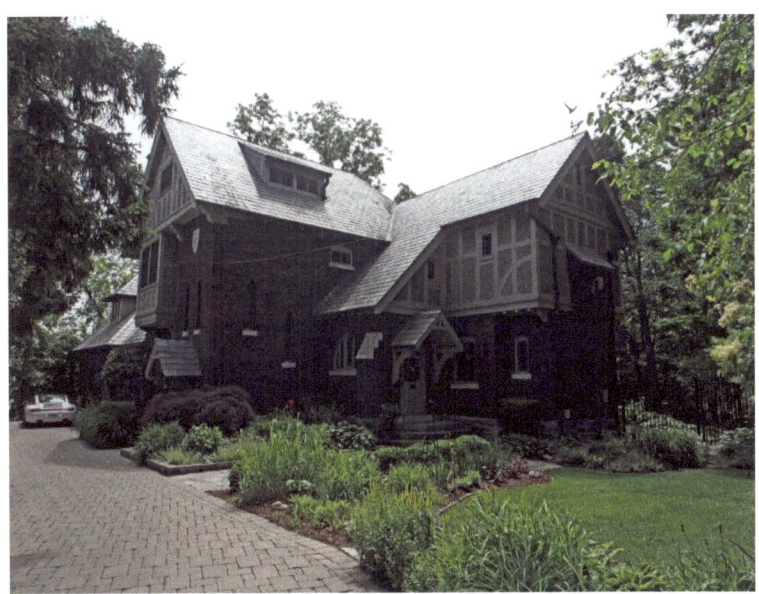

47 Albert Street – a Tudor Revival (Arts and Crafts) style house built in 1924 by the manager of the Globe Furniture Company, a world leader in furniture manufacturing especially church and school furnishings and religious carvings

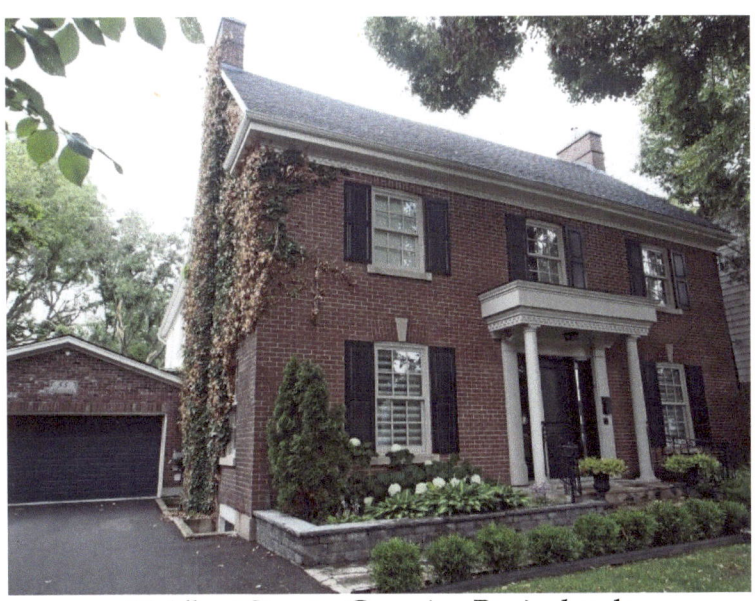

55 Albert Street – Georgian Revival style

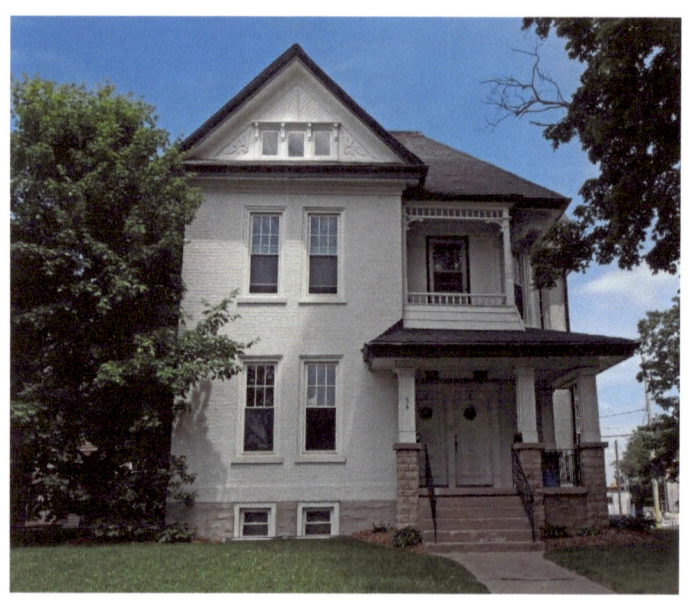

54 Albert Street – built in 1891 in the late Victorian Queen Anne style for Dr. Charles Noecker, the Medical Officer of Health; buff brick walls have been painted

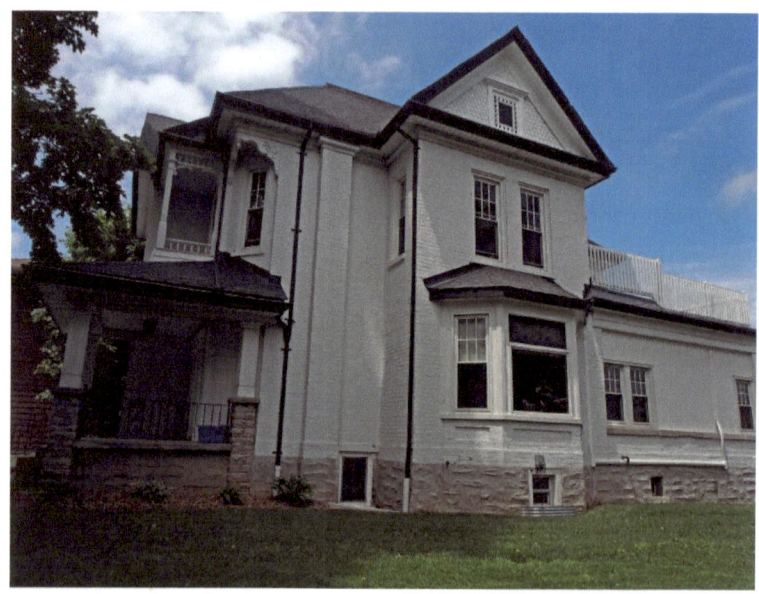

Fretwork, bay window, decorative gables

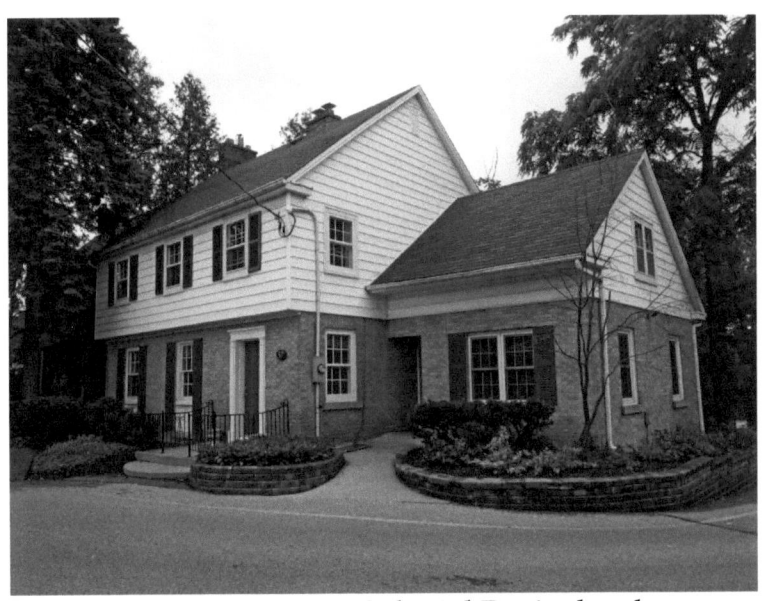

57 Albert Street – Colonial Revival style

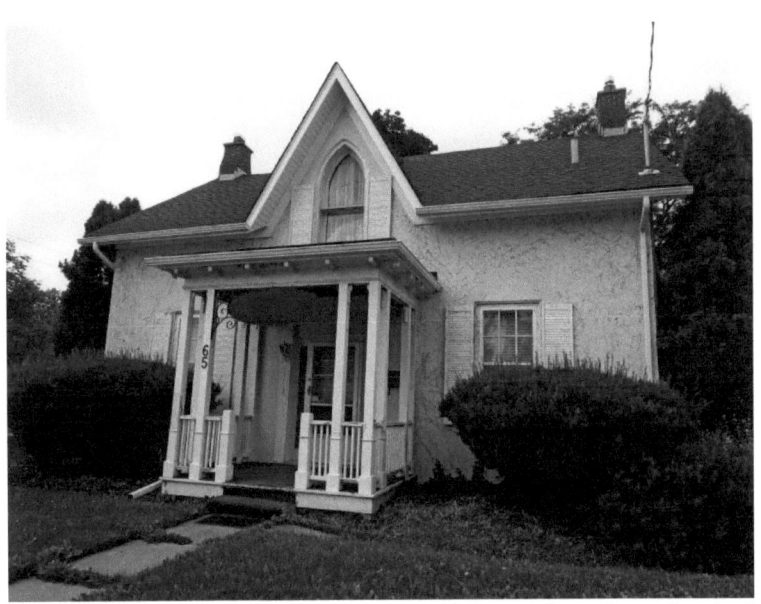

65 Albert Street – Gothic Revival, gable with pointed window,
Stucco over brick house built in 1866 by Elias Snider

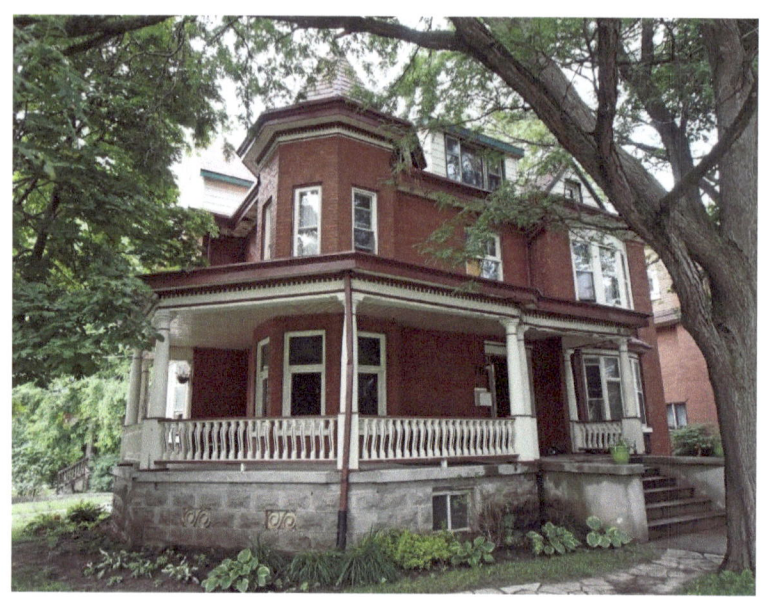

79 Albert Street – a Victorian Queen Anne style house built around 1907 – turret, wraparound verandah

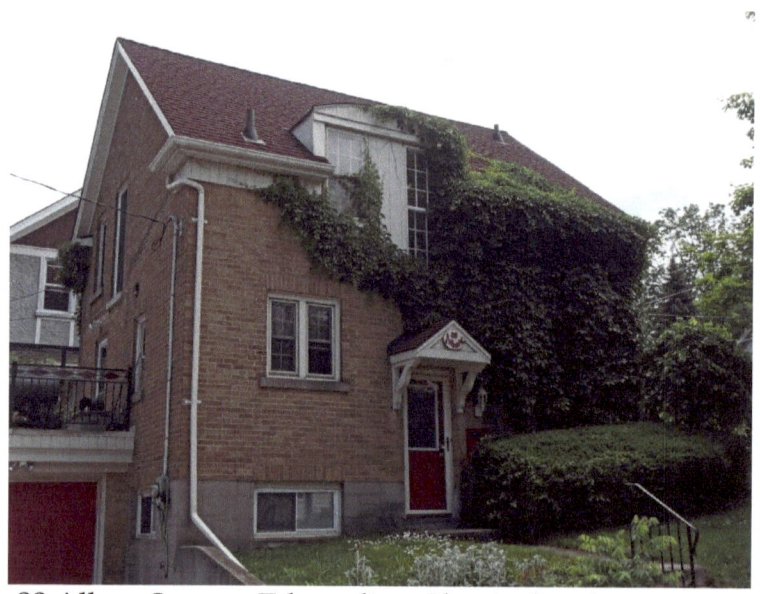

88 Albert Street – Edwardian Classical style variation

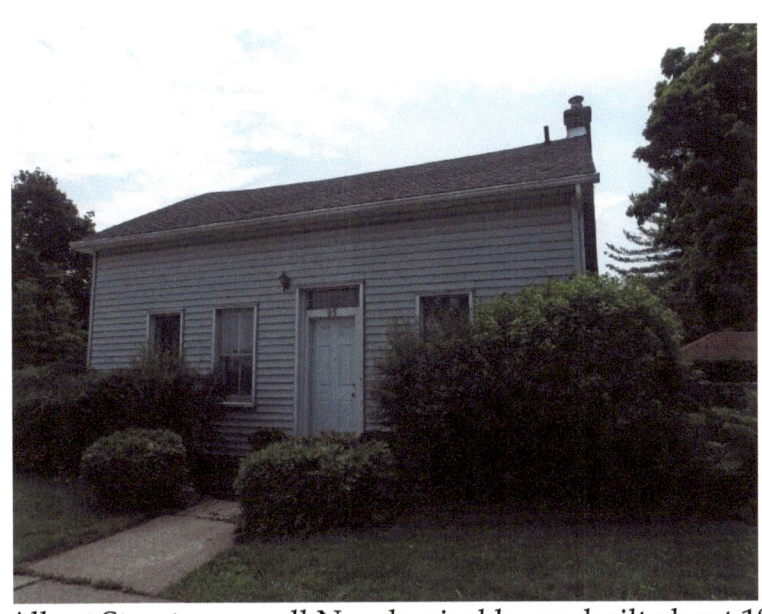

95 Albert Street – a small Neoclassical house built about 1880

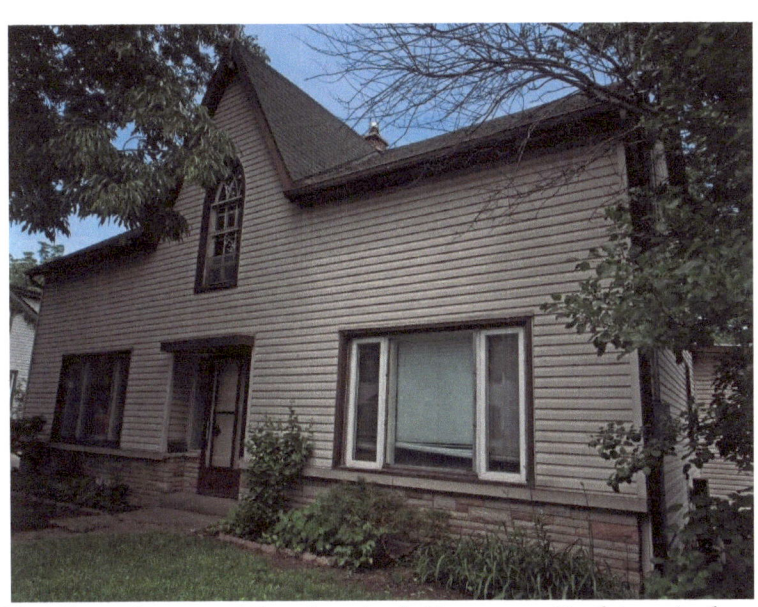

98 Albert Street – Neoclassical, Regency Gothic window,
finial in central peak

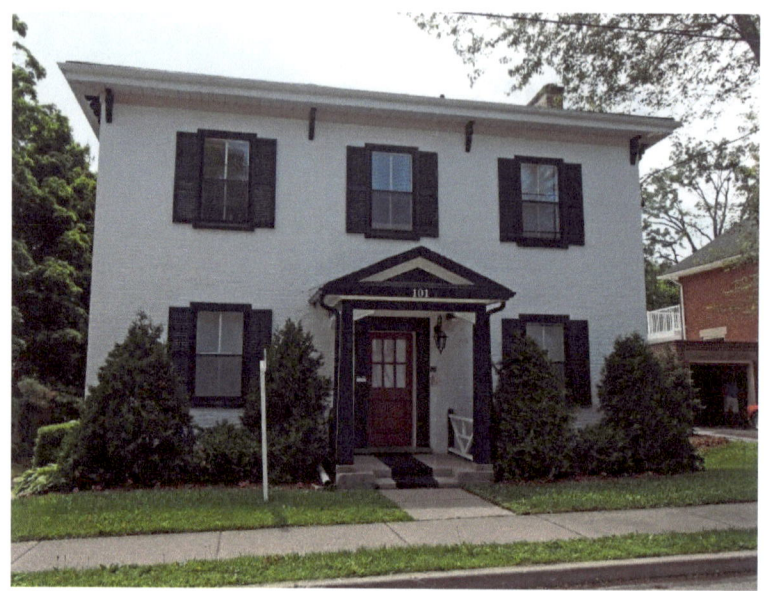

101 Albert Street – two storey Regency house with widely spaced Italianate cornice brackets under the eaves, pediment

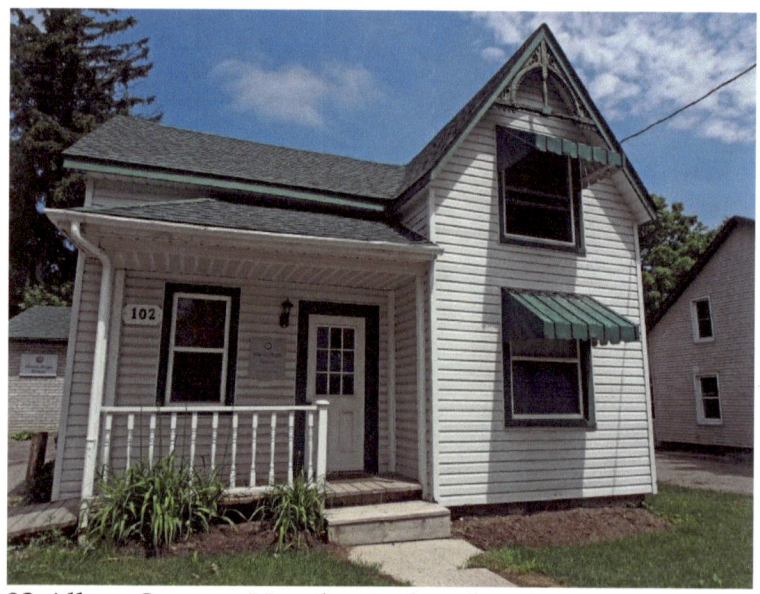

102 Albert Street – Neoclassical with a Queen Anne front addition, within the peak is a decorative arch with spindles

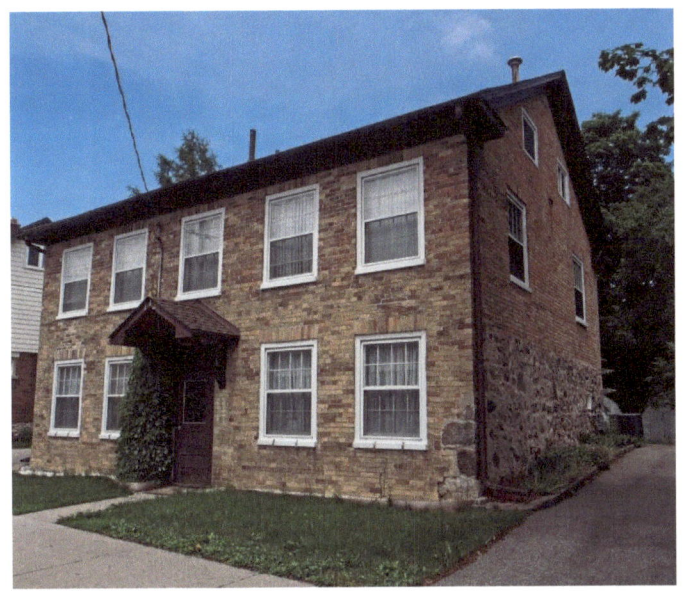

112 Albert Street – built in 1859 in the Mennonite Georgian style – a former hotel and tailor shop – buff brick with rubble stone lower wall, symmetrical front with five openings

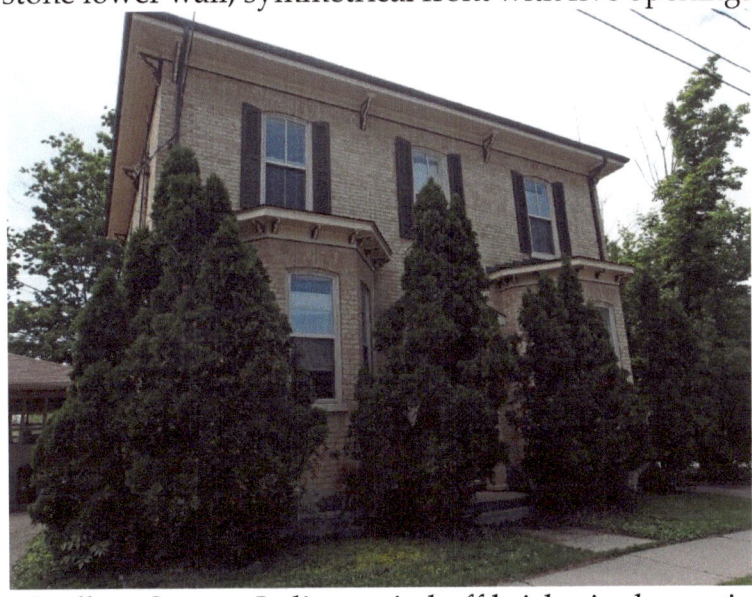

119 Albert Street – Italianate in buff brick, single cornice brackets, bay windows

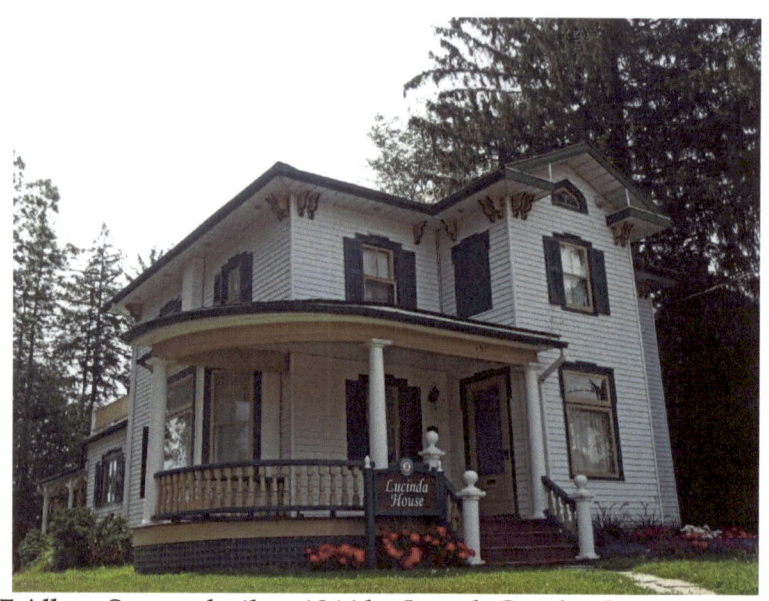

157 Albert Street – built c. 1846 by Joseph Good – Georgian style – moulded trim, shutters, eared window pediments, blind attic window, cornice return on front gable; modified by Allan Shantz in 1896 – semi-circular verandah with newel posts topped by cannon ball finials, stained glass parlour window – give late-Victorian appearance

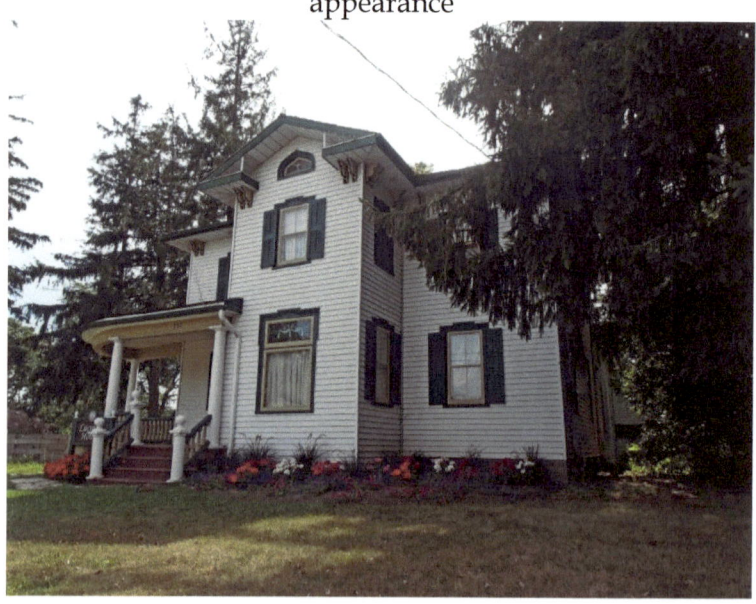

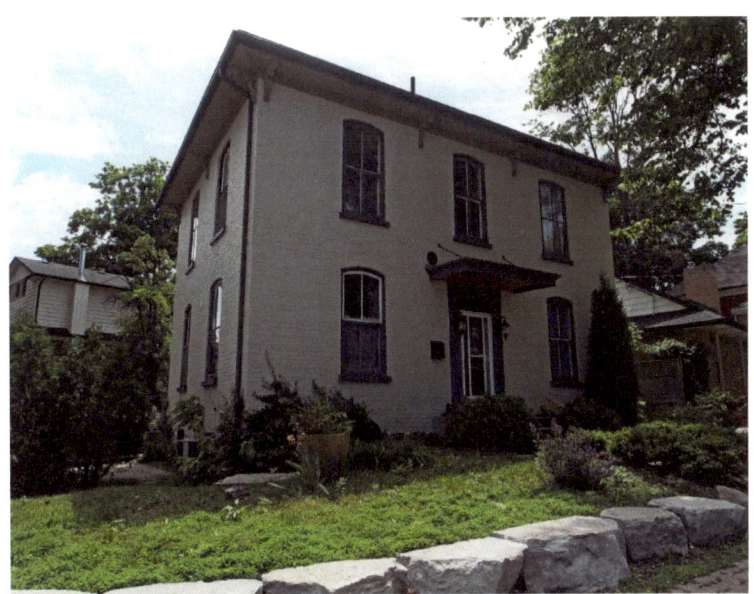

Albert Street – Italianate, cornice brackets

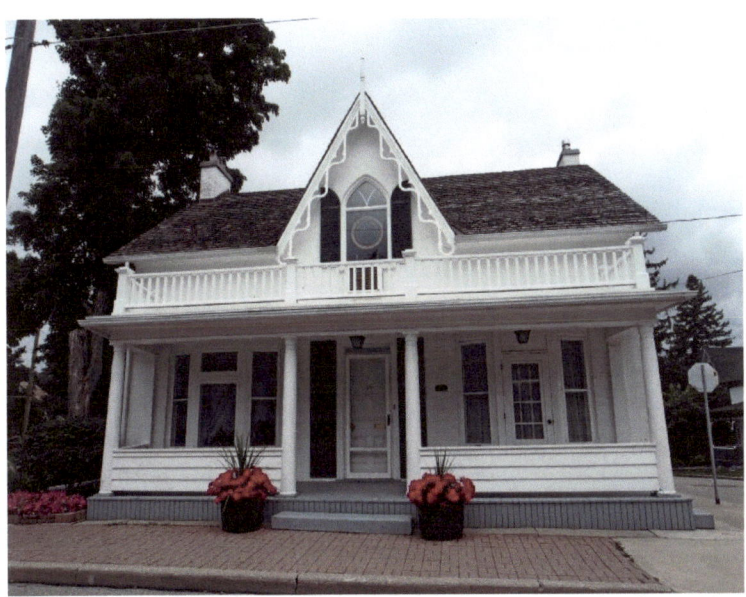

36 Young Street West – a former farmhouse on 300 acres built in 1849 – 1½ storey Gothic Revival style, gingerbread bargeboards and tall finial on the dormer, broken arch of the gable window, tripartite windows of the front façade – the small second front door gave access to the doctor's office

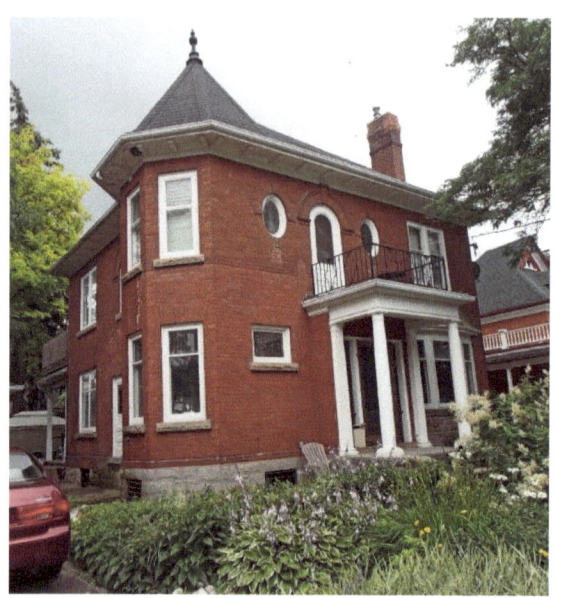

43 Young Street – Edwardian Classical house with turret, 2nd floor balcony

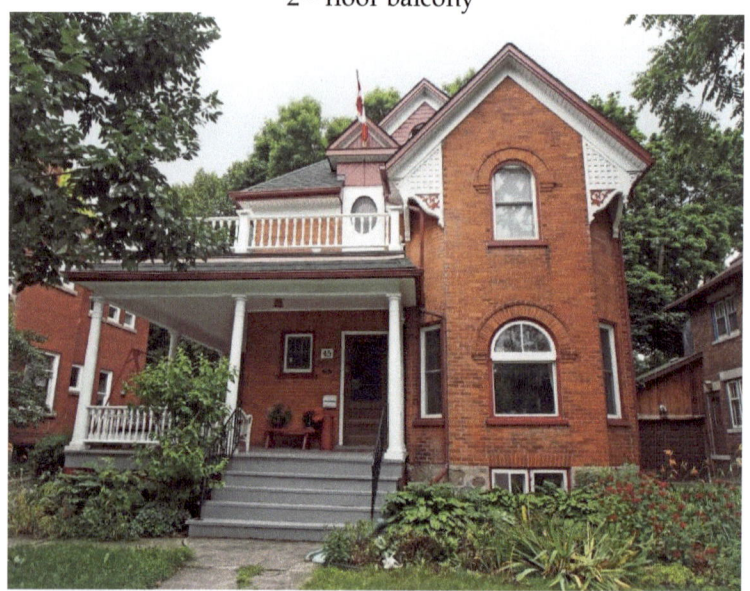

45 Young Street West – built in 1903 – Queen Anne style – made from local red clay bricks, irregular roofline with dormers and gables; fretwork brackets; wraparound verandah, second storey balcony

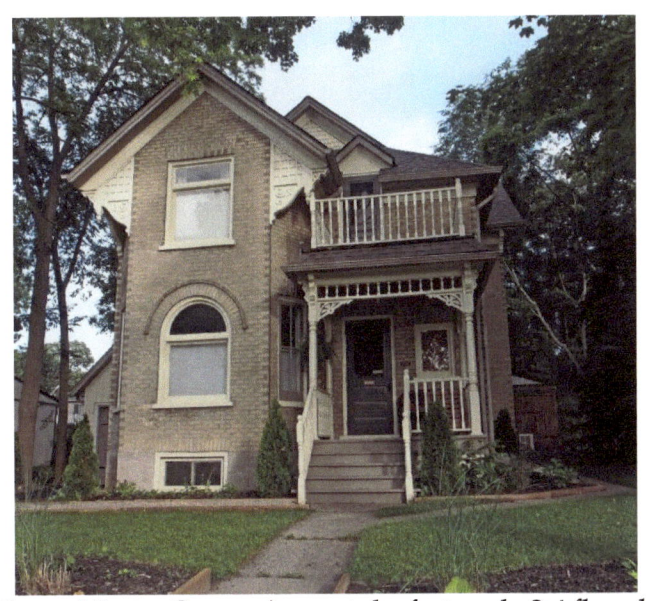

Young Street West – Queen Anne style, fretwork, 2nd floor balcony, arched window voussoirs

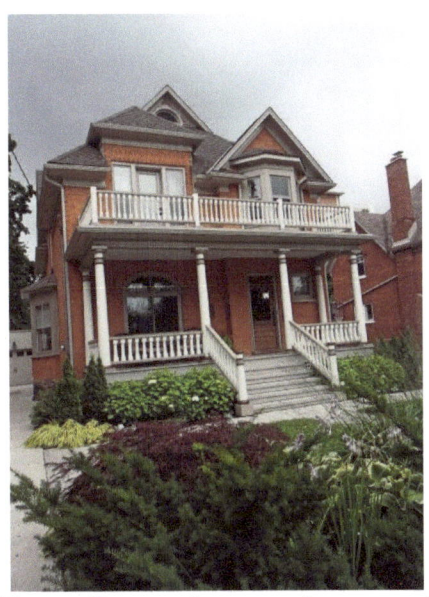

Young Street West – Queen Anne style, second floor balcony, bay window

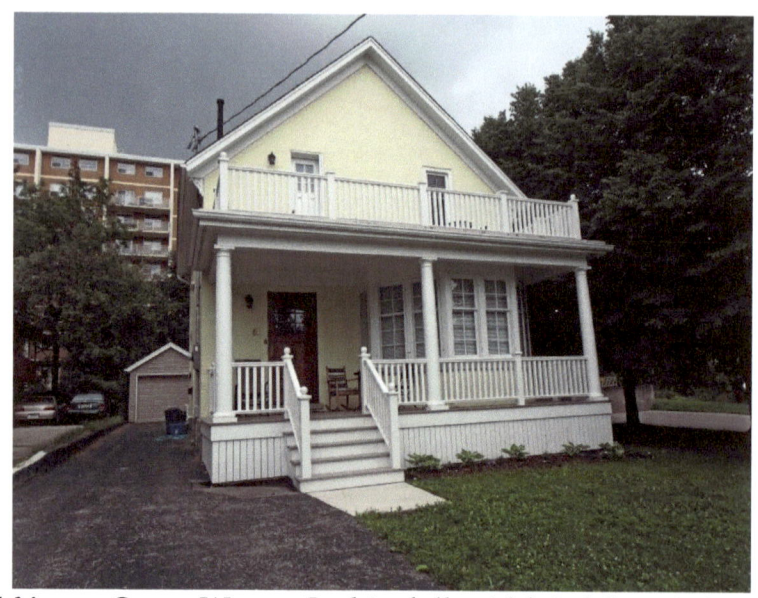

61 Young Street West – Gothic, full-width 2nd floor balcony, 1st floor bay window

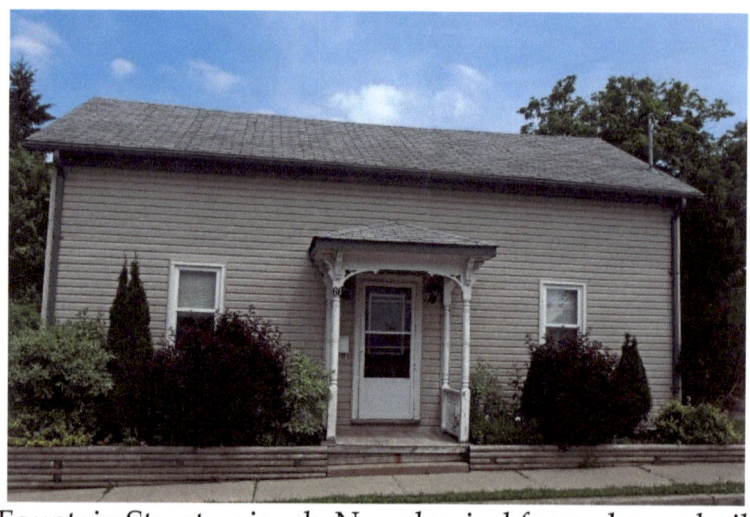

66 Fountain Street – simple Neo-classical frame house built in 1866 by John Schneider, a foreman for the Waterloo Manufacturing Company Limited

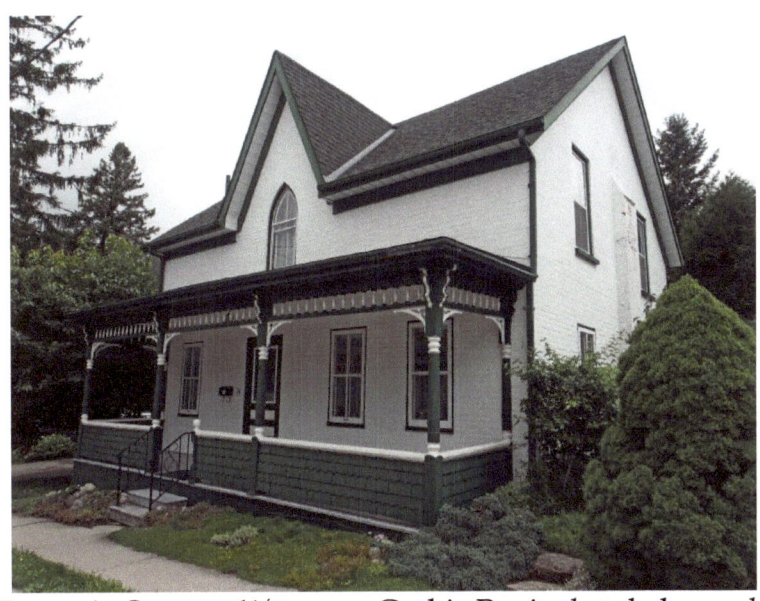

70 Fountain Street – 1½ storey Gothic Revival style house built
in 1876, delicate wood-turned verandah sets off
the front facade

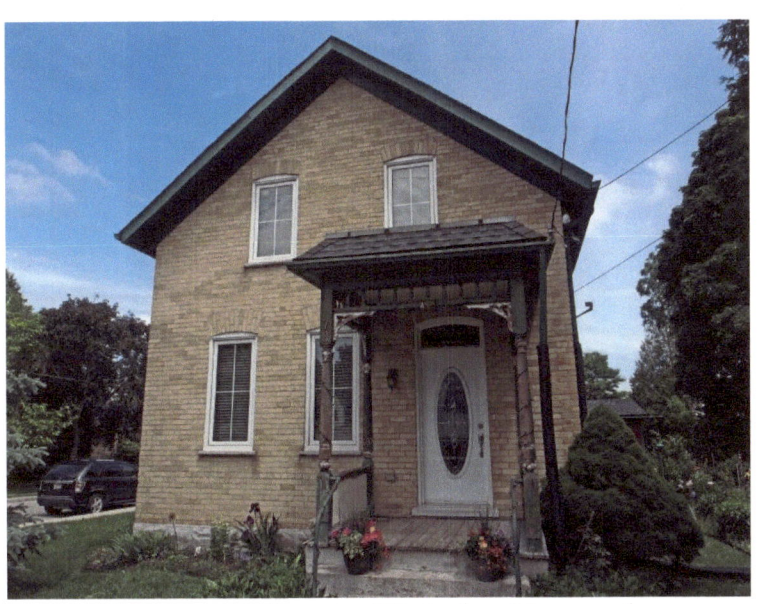

78 Fountain Street – Waterloo Vernacular

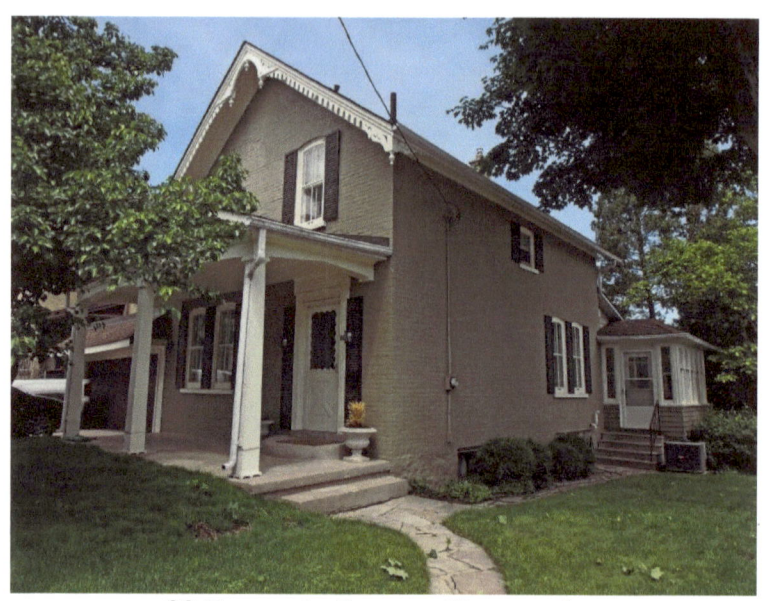

80 Fountain Street – Vernacular

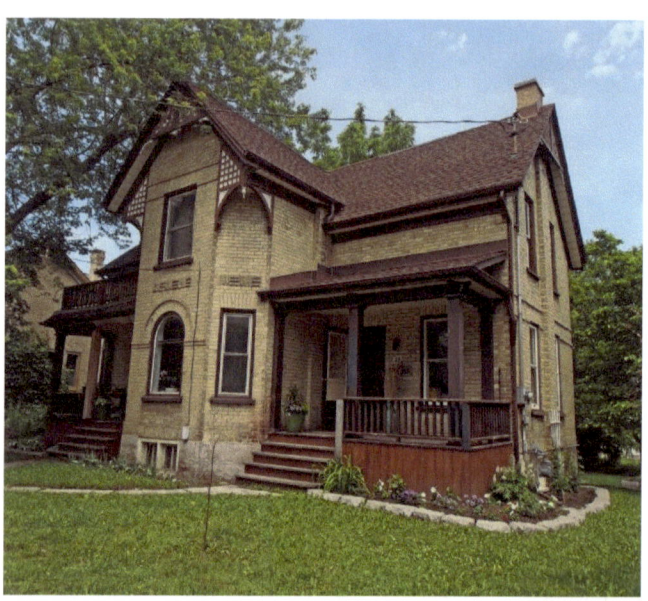

86 Fountain Street – Queen Anne – fretwork

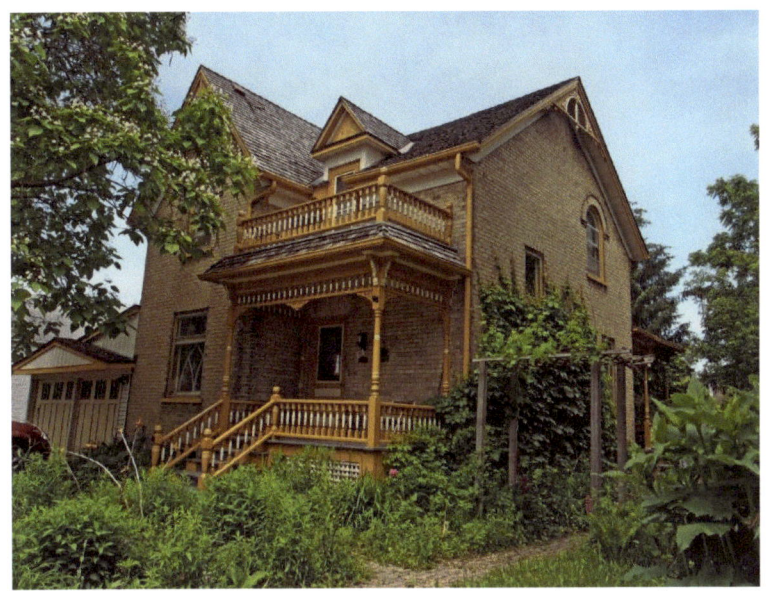

88 Fountain Street – 1¾ storey height, Queen Anne style – yellow brick, rubble stone foundation, projecting rectangular bay, turned verandah roof supports, delicate spindles, intricately detailed woodwork; within peak of each gable is a decorative arch with applied scrollwork, spindles & circular piercing; 2nd storey windows are semicircular at top; dormer gives access to upper porch

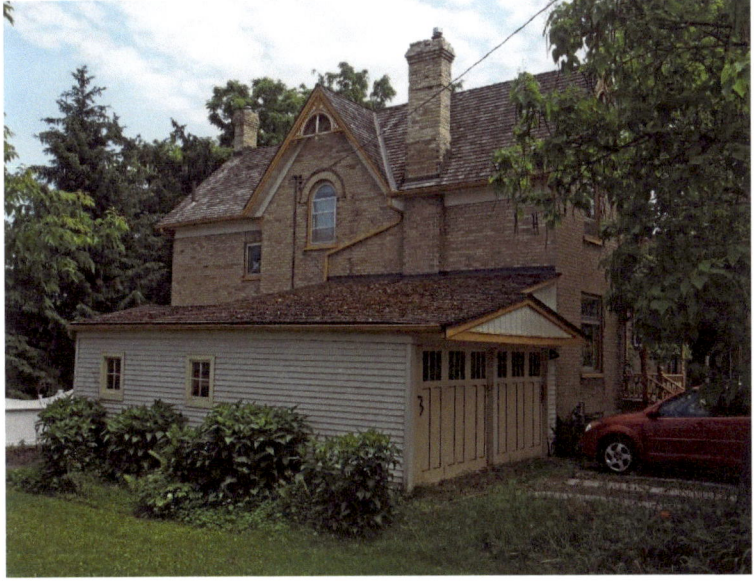

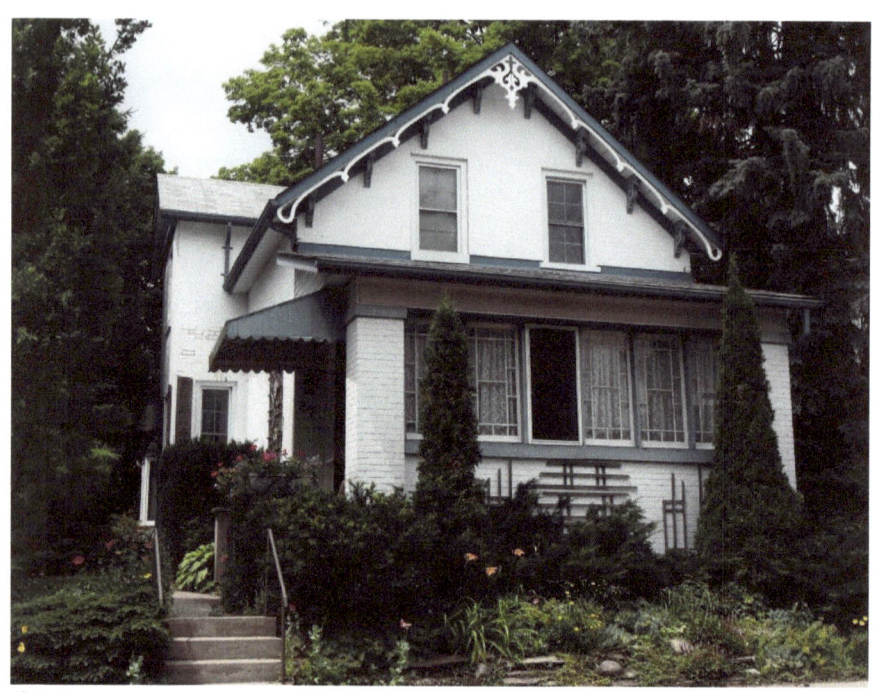

87 Fountain Street – Gothic Revival, bargeboard trim on gable

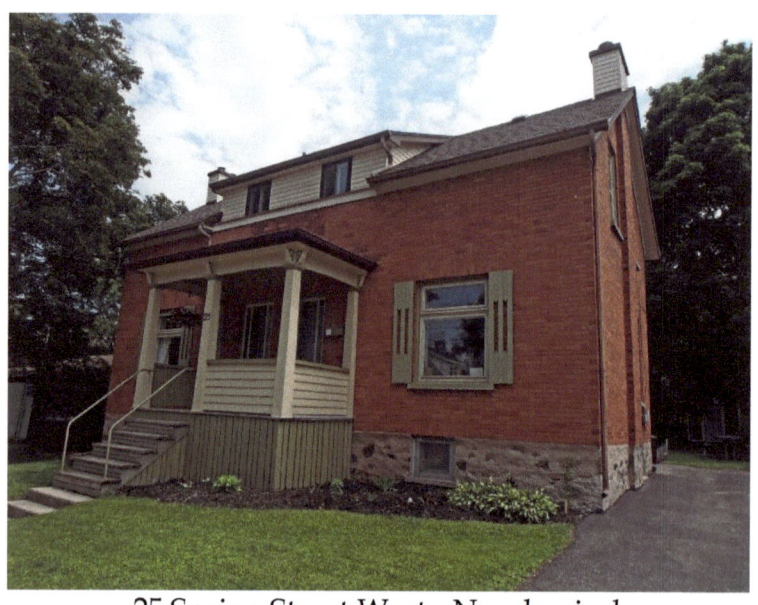

25 Spring Street West - Neoclassical

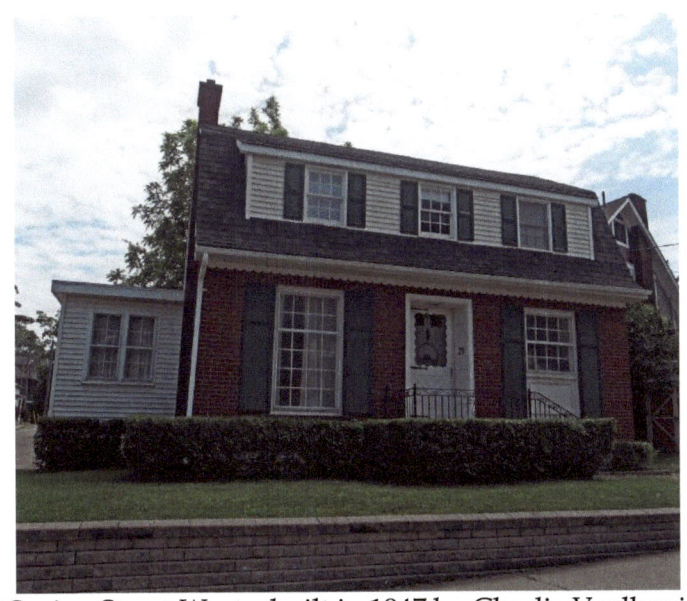

29 Spring Street West – built in 1947 by Charlie Voelker in a Neocolonial style in red rug-brick veneer with vinyl siding on the gable ends, sunroom and dormers; each of its elevations is symmetrical; gambrel roof with shed dormers in the Dutch style, nearly as wide as the house, at the front and rear; scalloping on the façade's frieze; very large windows in the lower front facade

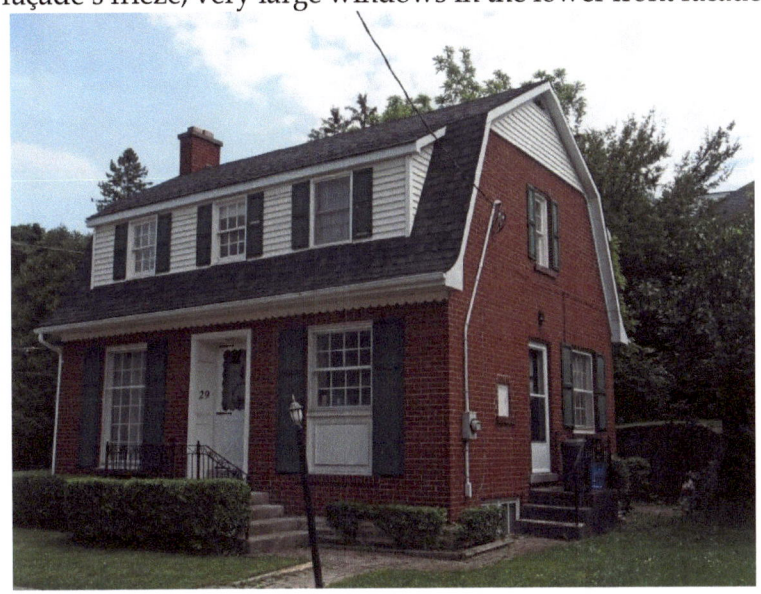

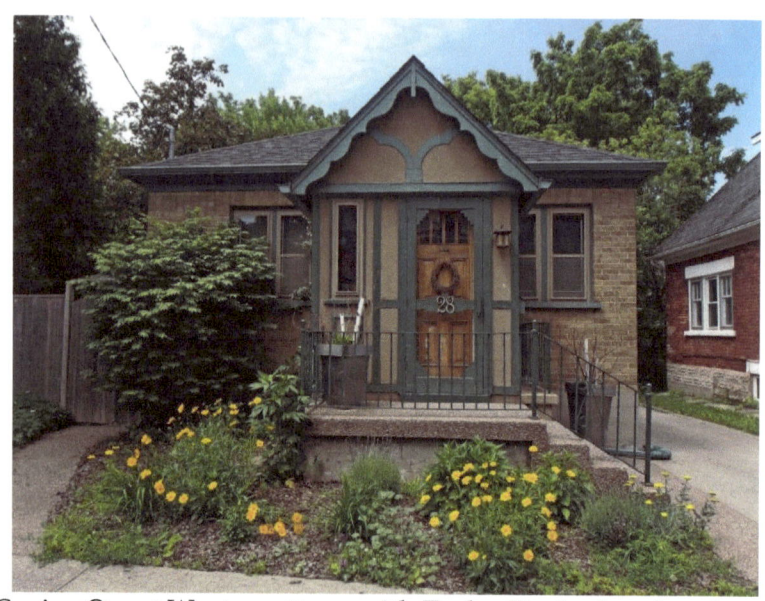

28 Spring Street West – cottage with Tudor Revival enclosed porch, verge board and finial on gable

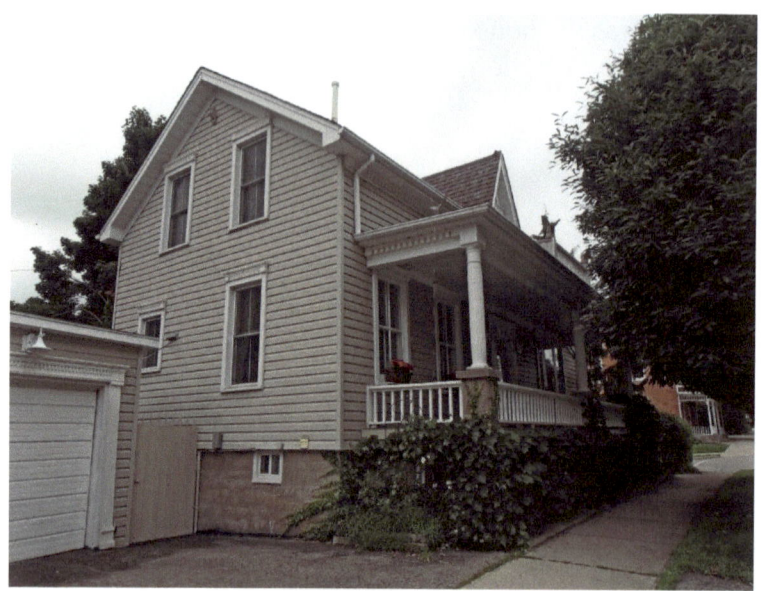

Central Street

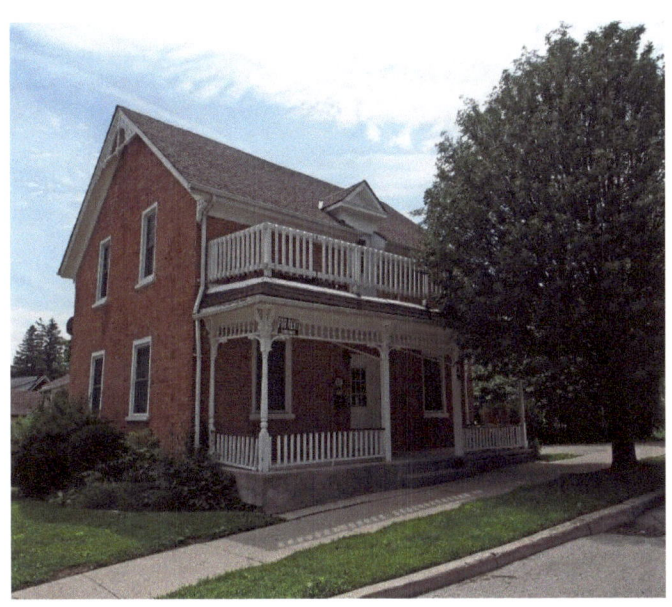

17 Central Street – Gothic Revival – built in 1866 – bargeboard in the peak on the gable end wall with spindles, wooden trim under porch roof, 2nd floor balcony, small central peak at front

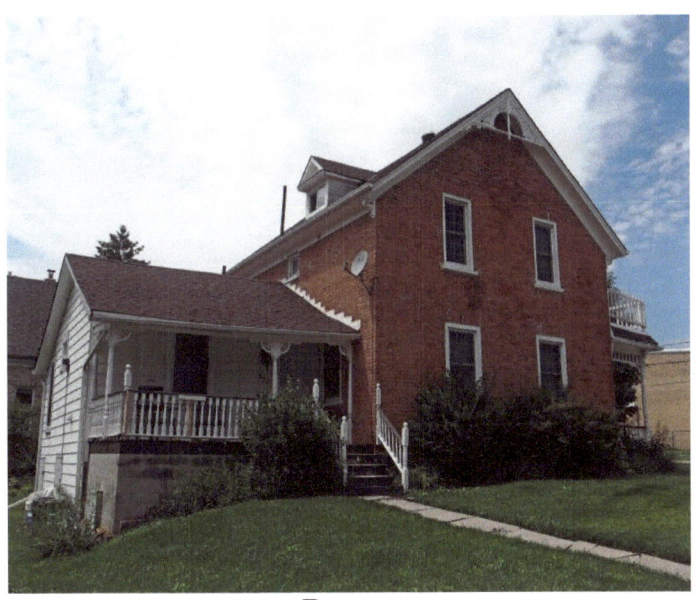

Dormer

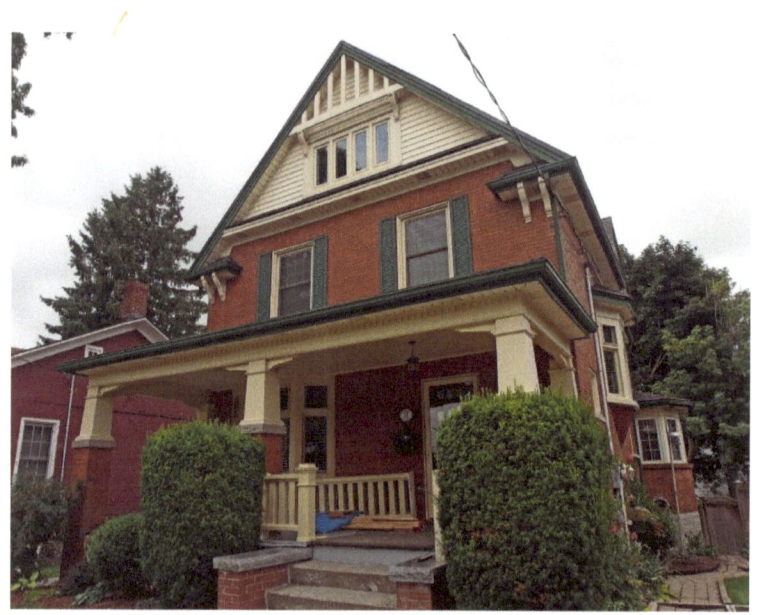

11 Central Street – Edwardian Classical, cornice brackets on cornice return of gable, side bay windows

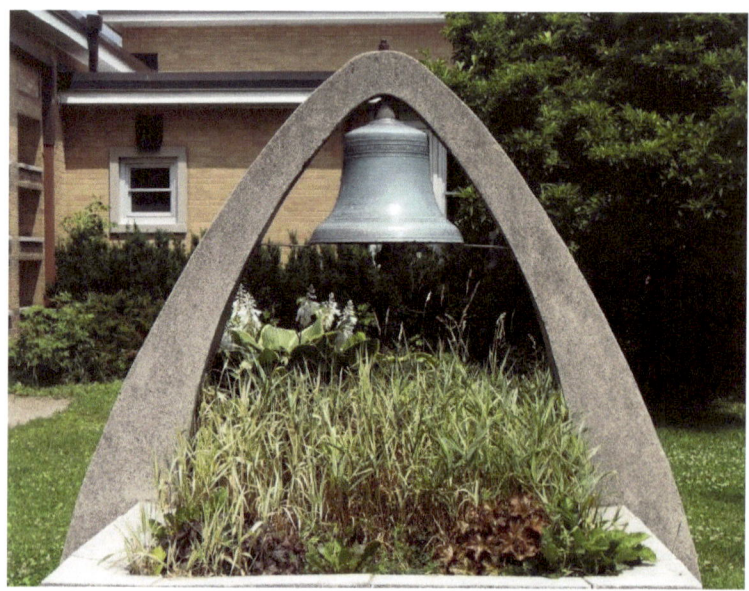

The 1st school bell in Waterloo place on Central School built in 1855

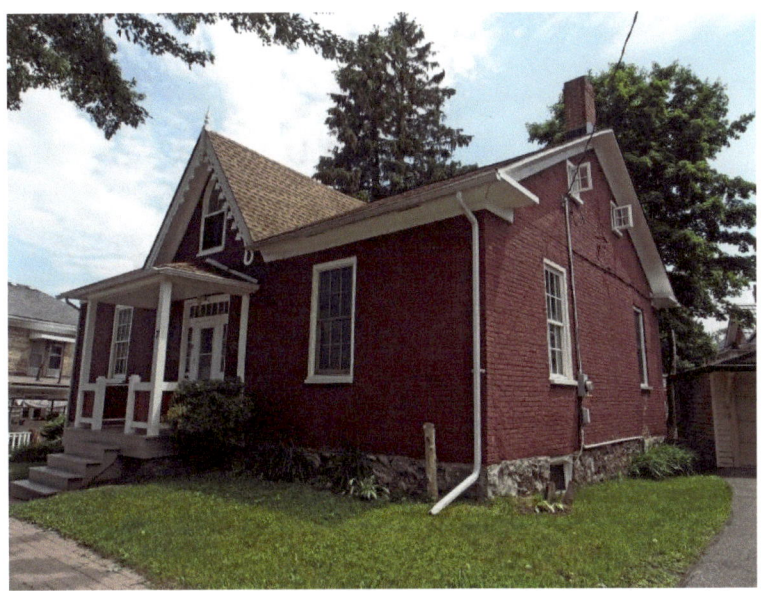

7 Central Street – built 1849 in the Georgian style (symmetrical front façade, central doorway, transom, sidelights, cornice returns on the eaves and two pairs of small attic windows) by Samuel Burkholder, a Pennsylvania mason and bricklayer – the local Evangelical congregation used it for meetings and worhsip.  In 1870 it was converterted to a dwelling with addition of Gothic elements - gable above the entrance with decorative bargeboard and Gothic window.

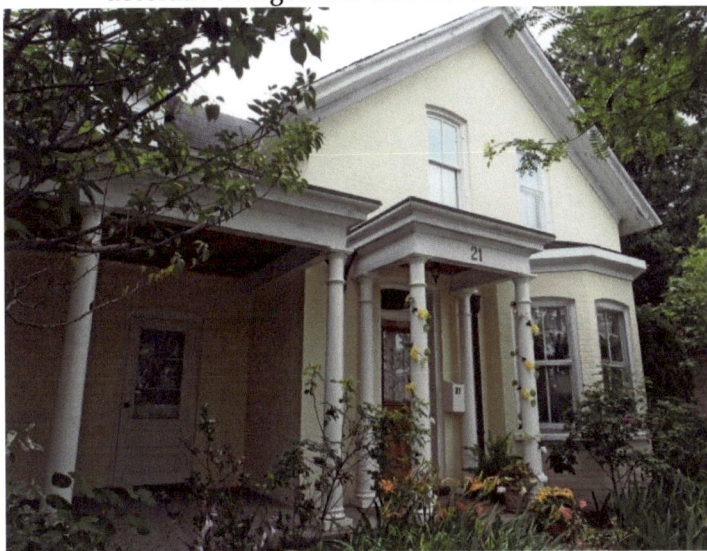

21 Central Street – Gothic Revival of the High Victorian era, bay window

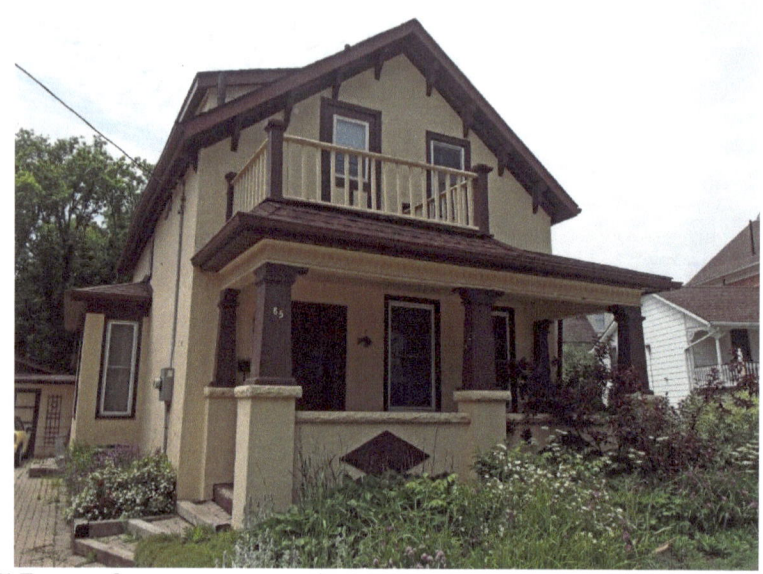

85 Dorset Street – Vernacular, 2nd floor balcony, cornice brackets

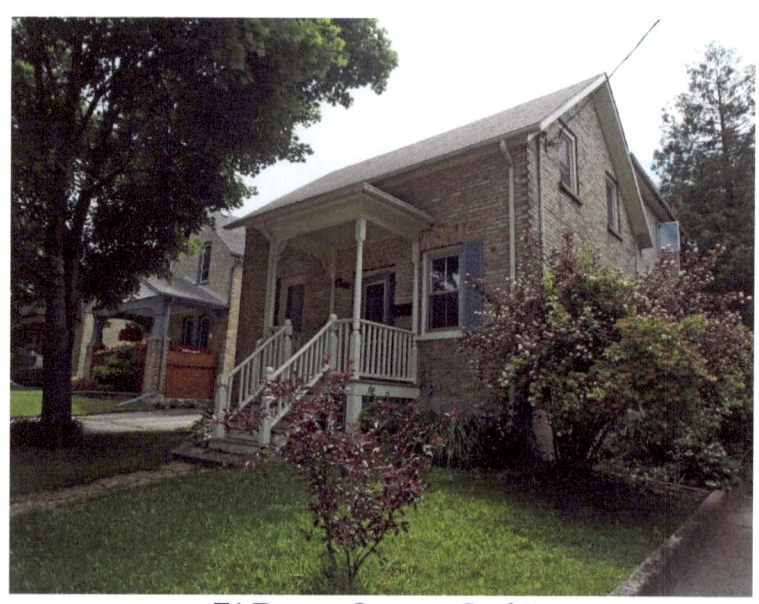

74 Dorset Street - Gothic

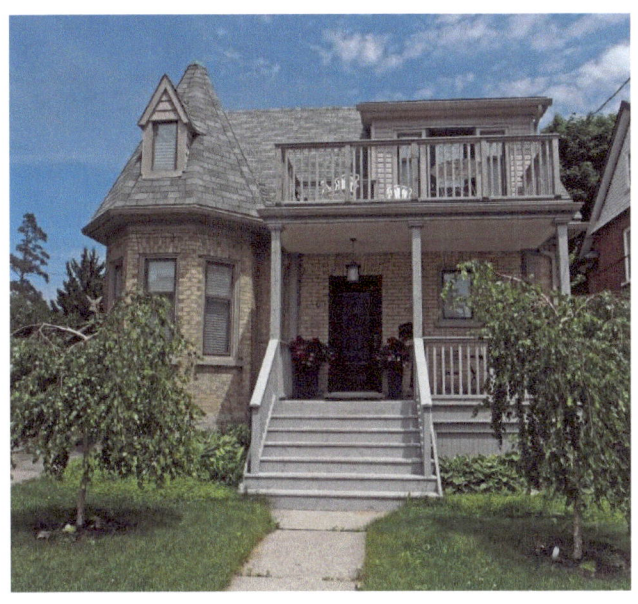

84 Dorset Street – Queen Anne style, turret, 2nd floor balcony

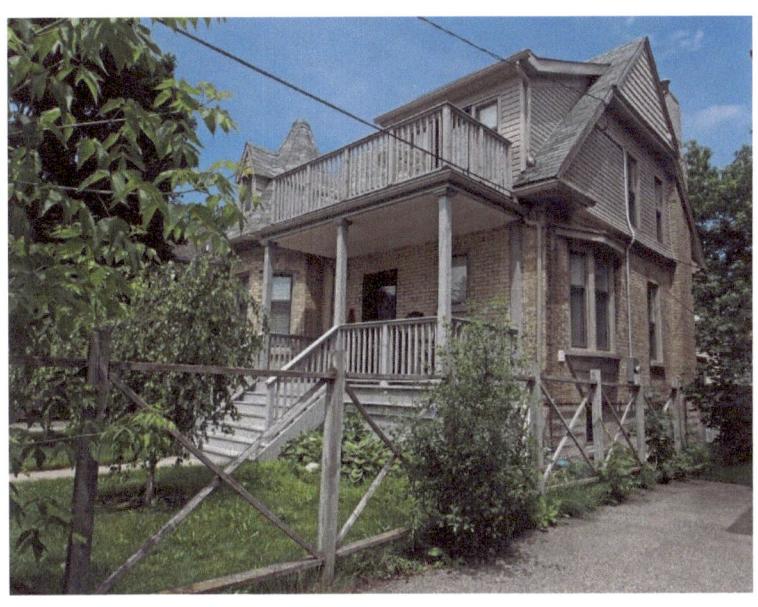

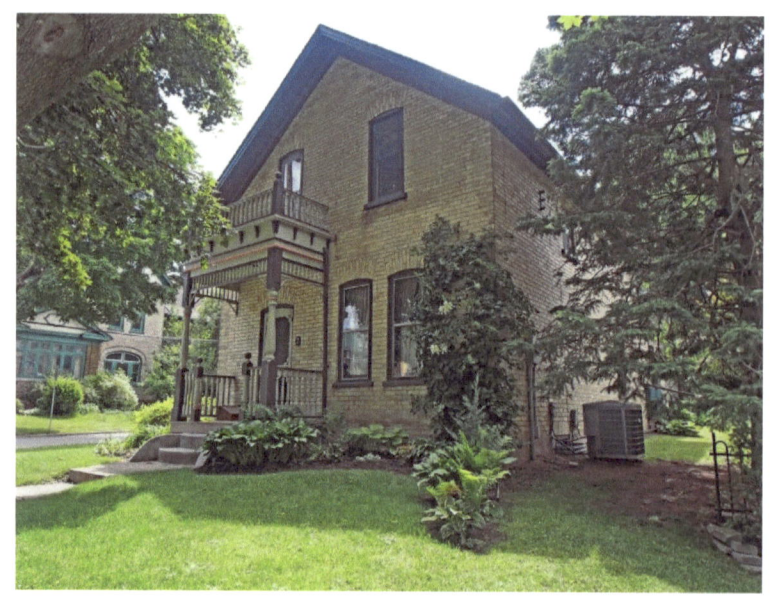

63 Dorset Street – Vernacular, 2nd floor balcony – built 1886

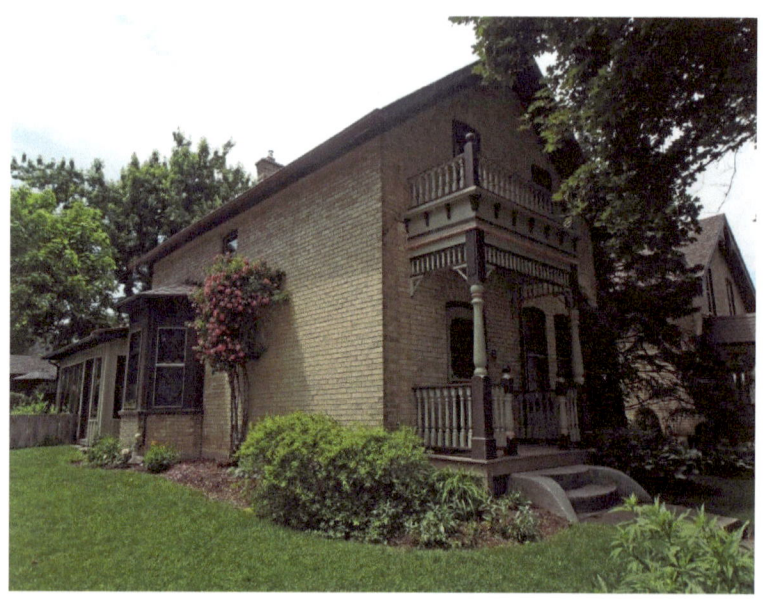

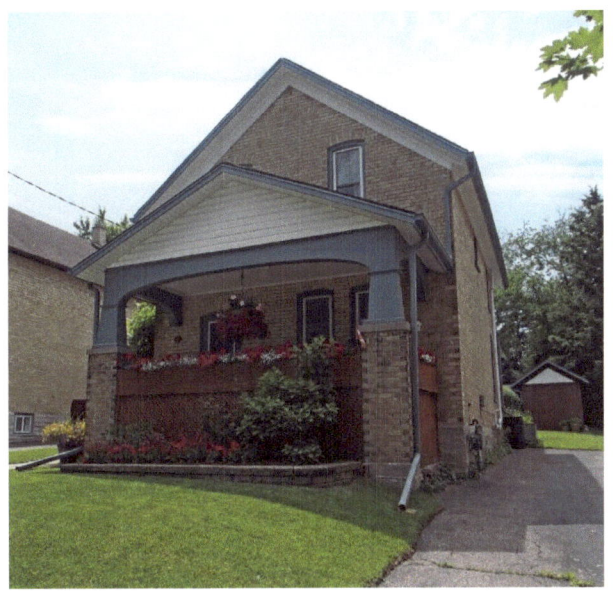

69 Dorset Street – Vernacular – built in 1886

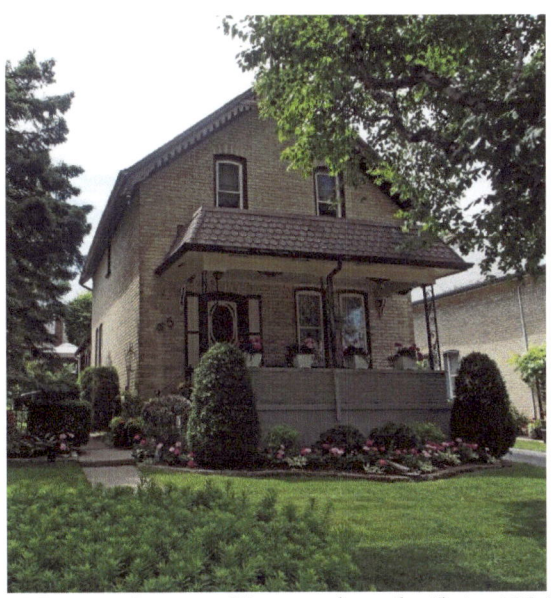

65 Dorset Street – Vernacular – built in 1886

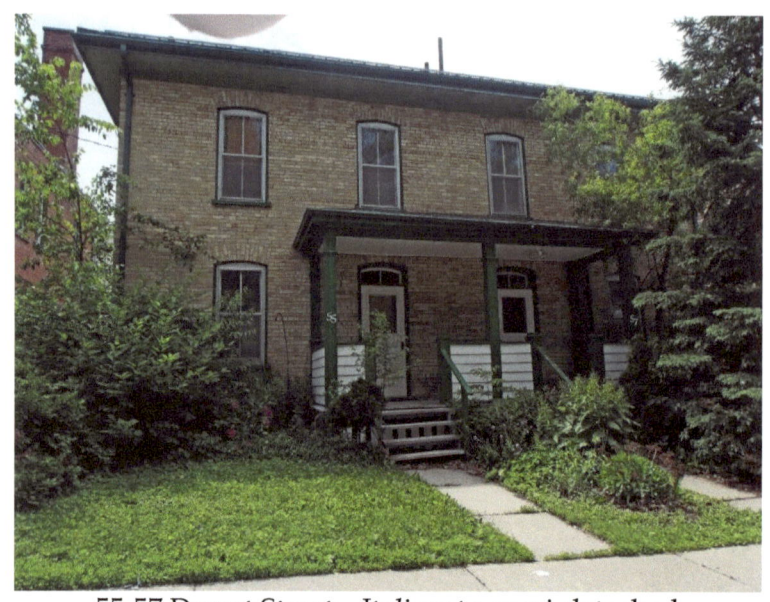

55-57 Dorset Street – Italianate, semi-detached

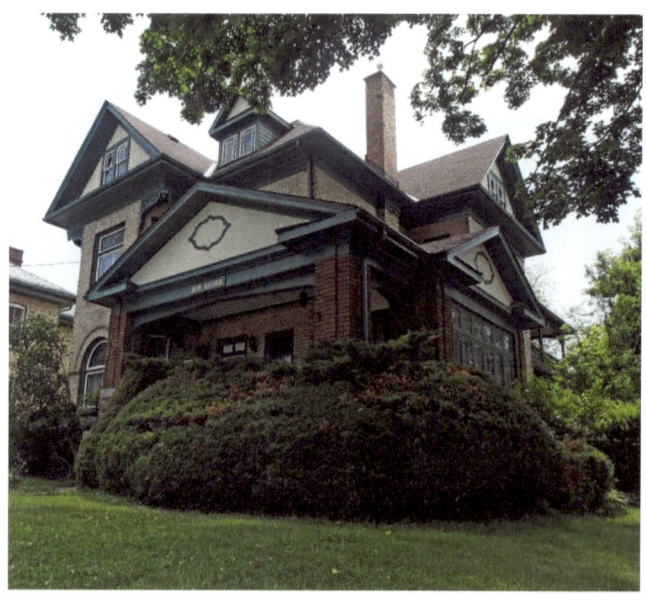

61 Dorset Street – varied roof line, two street fronts

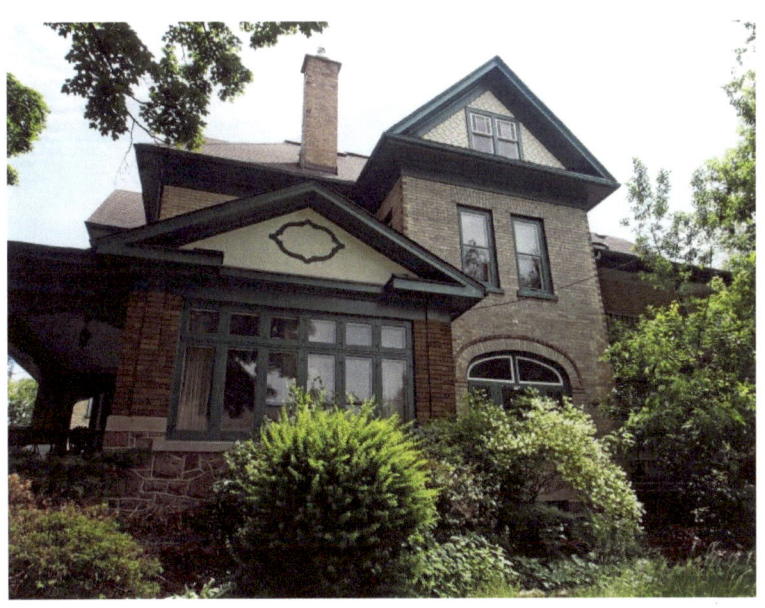

61 Dorset Street – "Bon Accord" – Victorian Queen Anne style built in 1898, stained glass windows, Romanesque style window arches on ground floor windows

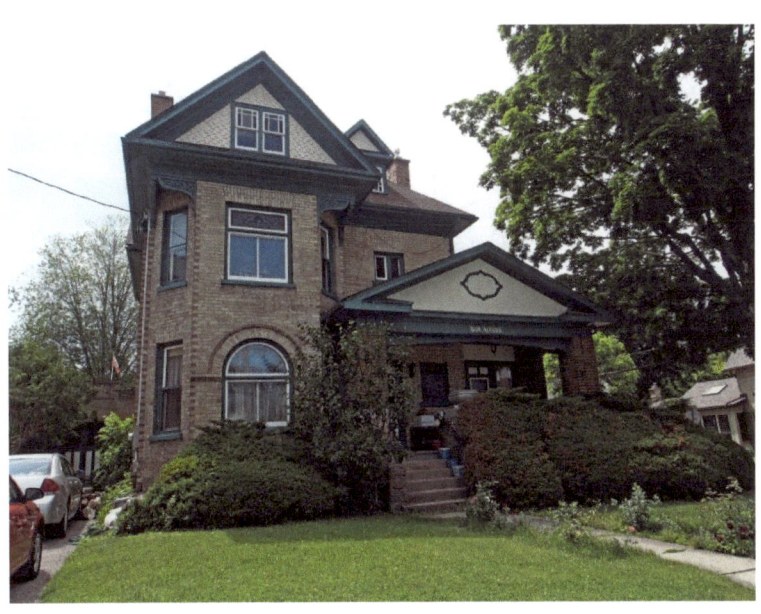

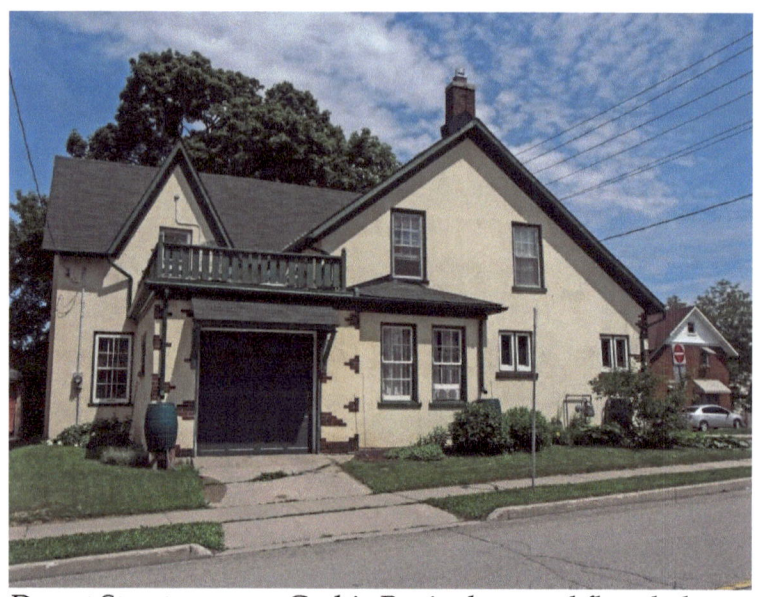

Dorset Street corner – Gothic Revival, second floor balcony

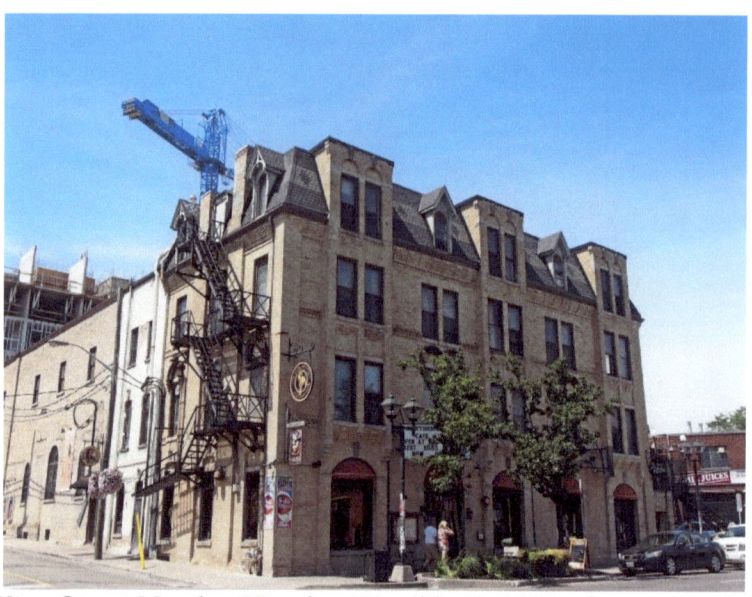

59 King Street North – Heuther Hotel built 1842 – four storey brick
and stone – Victorian style – dormers with window hoods – the
King Street façade was added in 1880

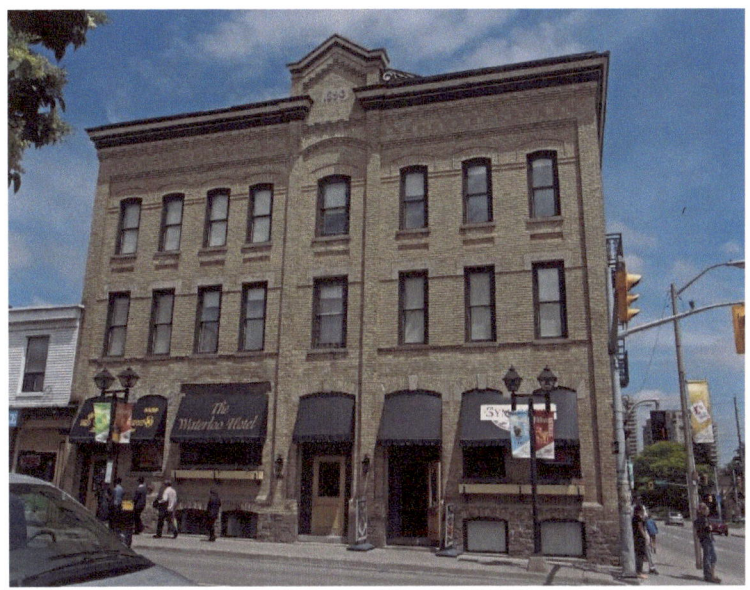

4 King Street North – The Waterloo Hotel - 1890 Inn – thirty bedrooms -
sand-colored brick in a Victorian style with a central pointed Grecian-style
pediment crowning the date stone which rises above the building's
projecting wood cornice; dentil moulding; 1st level arched brick lintels with
keystones, 2nd level solid stone Soldier lintels, 3rd level brick arches without
keystones; rough-cut stone ashlar foundation

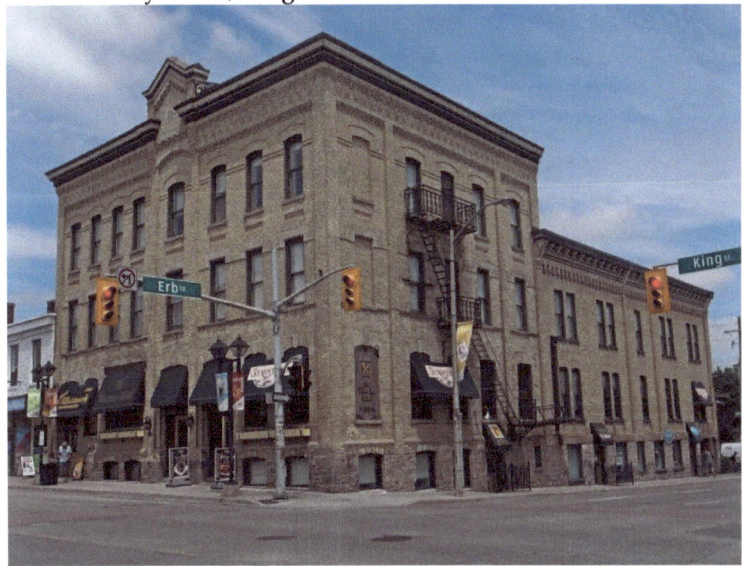

Fire escapes and Erb Street railings feature intricate wrought-iron metal
work; Erb Street parapet; cornice brackets

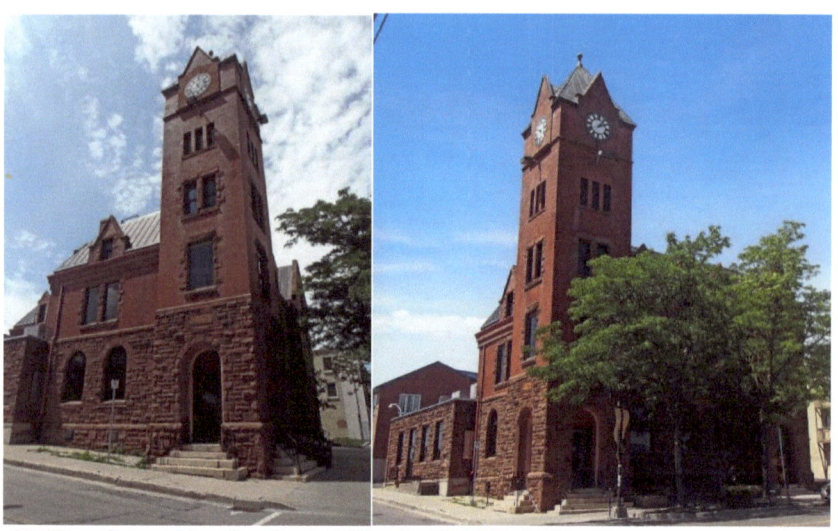

35 King Street North – Post Office built 1911-1913 – Romanesque style – rusticated sandstone on ground floor and around upper floor windows; red brick for upper floors; semicircular arches for windows and entranceways (lowest level); on the top storey, a steeply sloped copper-clad face over two corbelled courses of stone, and tall, stone dormers below a flat roof; corner clock tower with pediment

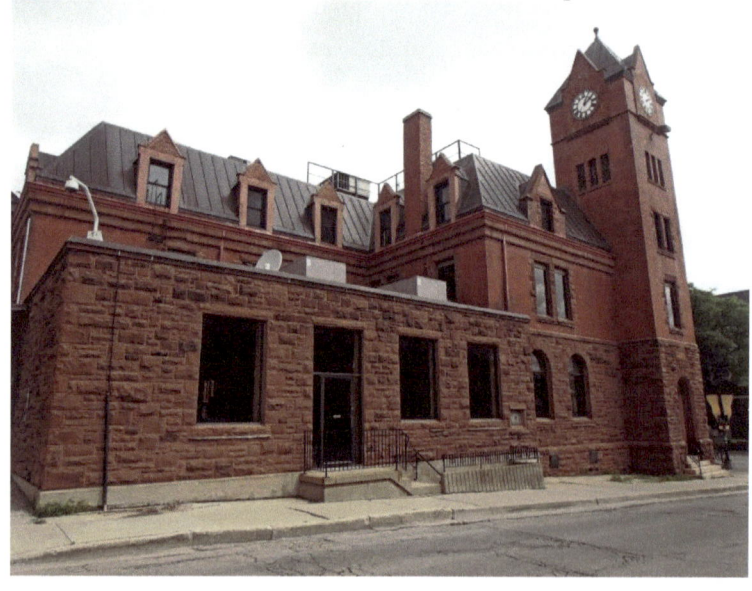

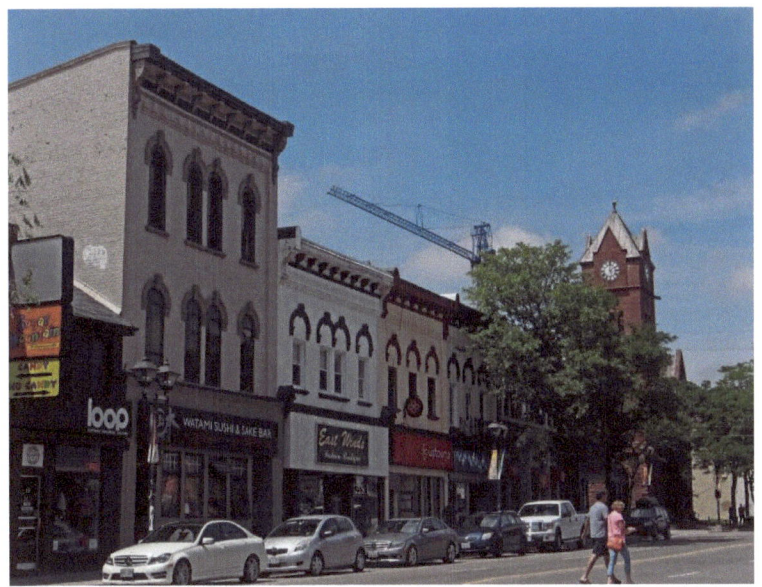

King Street North

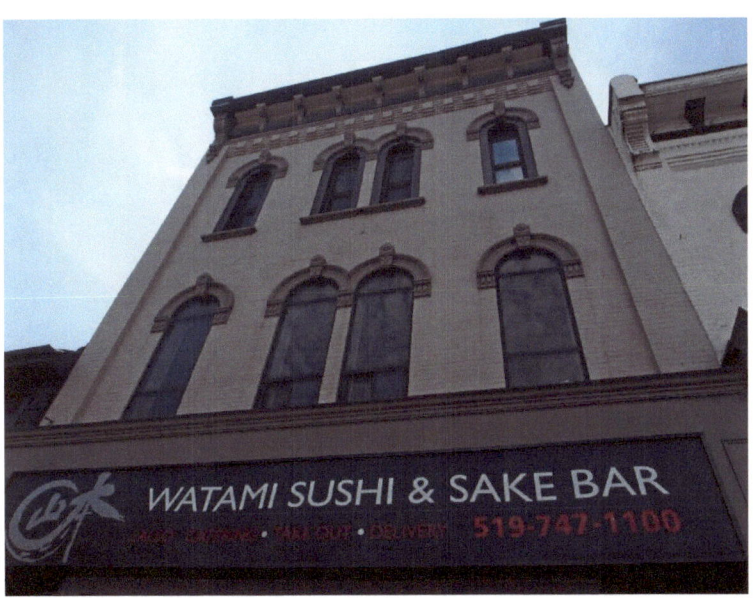

15 King Street North – built 1869 – arches over windows with
keystones, bevelled dentil moulding, cornice brackets

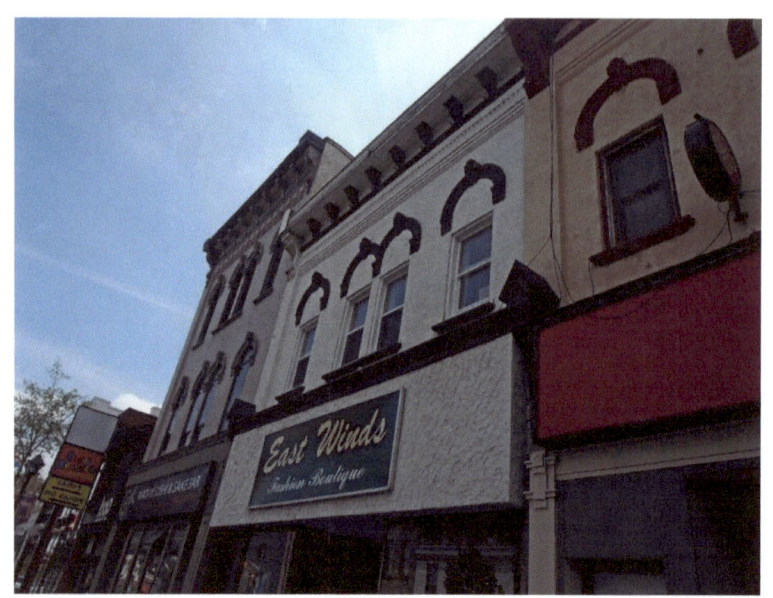

King Street North – arched window voussoirs with keystones, cornice brackets – built in 1869

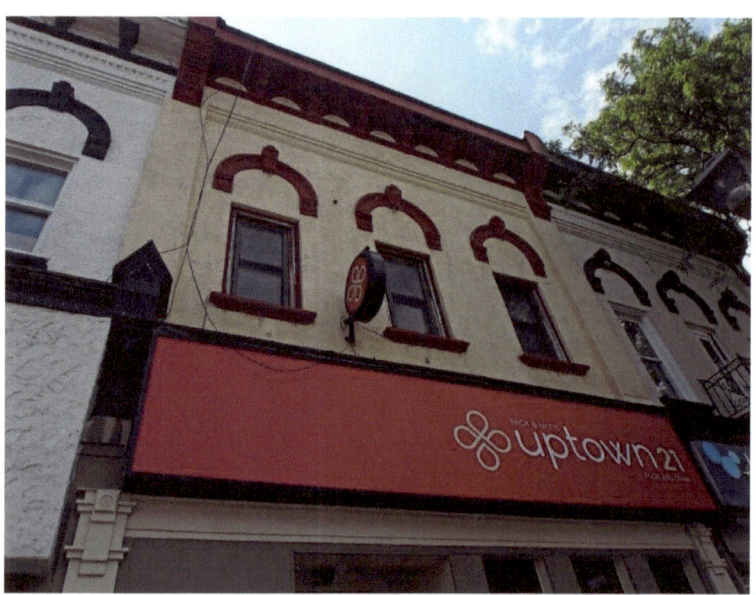

21 King Street North – built in 1869

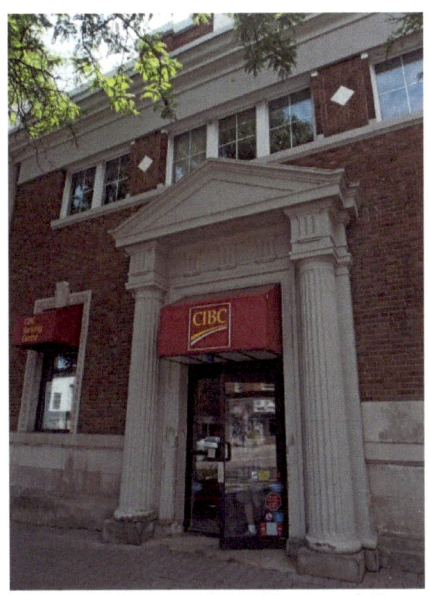

27 King Street North – CIBC Bank – Classical Revival style portico, decorative brickwork between windows – built 1914

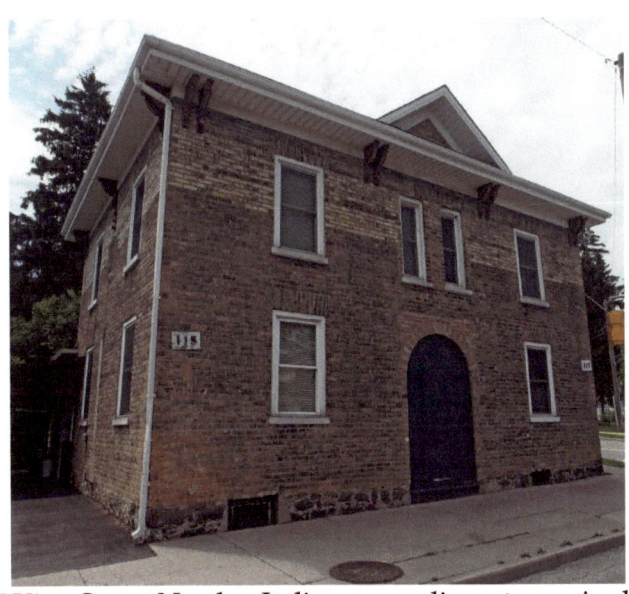

115-117 King Street North – Italianate, pediment, cornice brackets

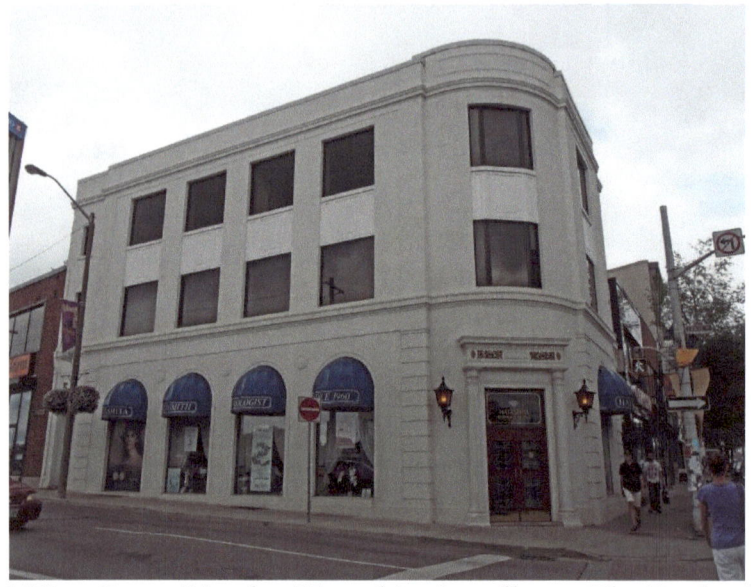

1 King Street North – Hatashita Jewellers – The Bank of Toronto built the present Art Deco style building in 1924

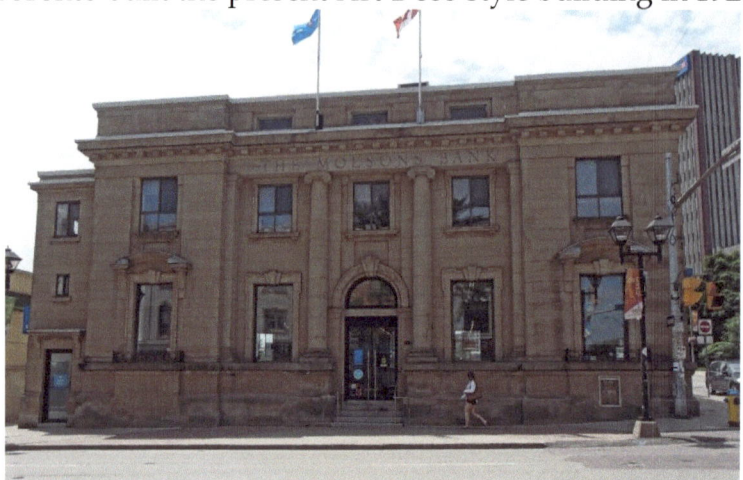

3 King Street South – built in 1914 – The Bank of Montreal, formerly The Molson's Bank – classical bank architecture in Beaux Arts style – a plinth identified by a heavy moulding, symmetrical main front façade, engaged Ionic columns, recessed doorway, keystones over the windows, half round door transom, curved stone pediments over two windows, and architrave with building's name engraved, cornice carried on dentils – all is dressed in cut stone a sober grey

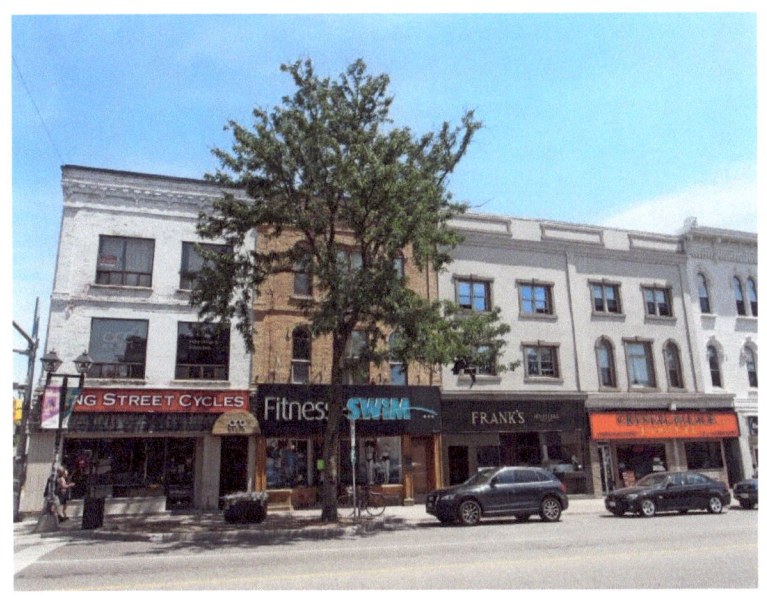

2-8 King Street South – commercial block 1861

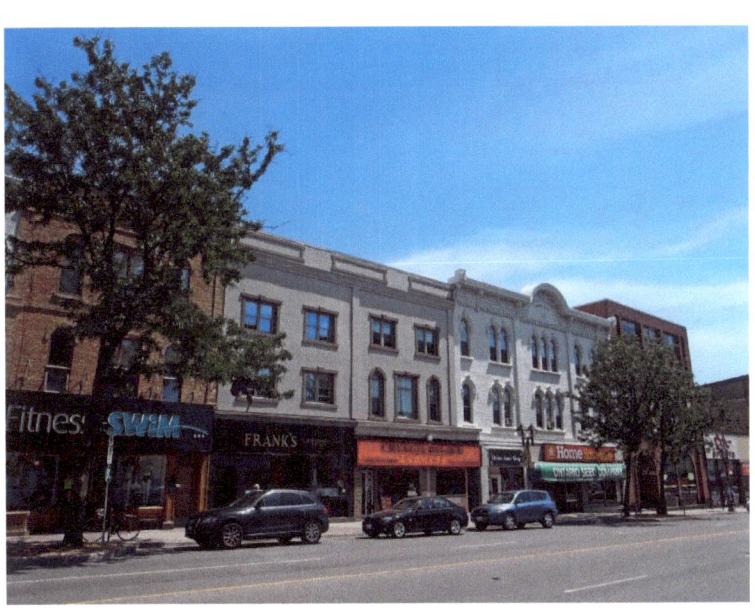

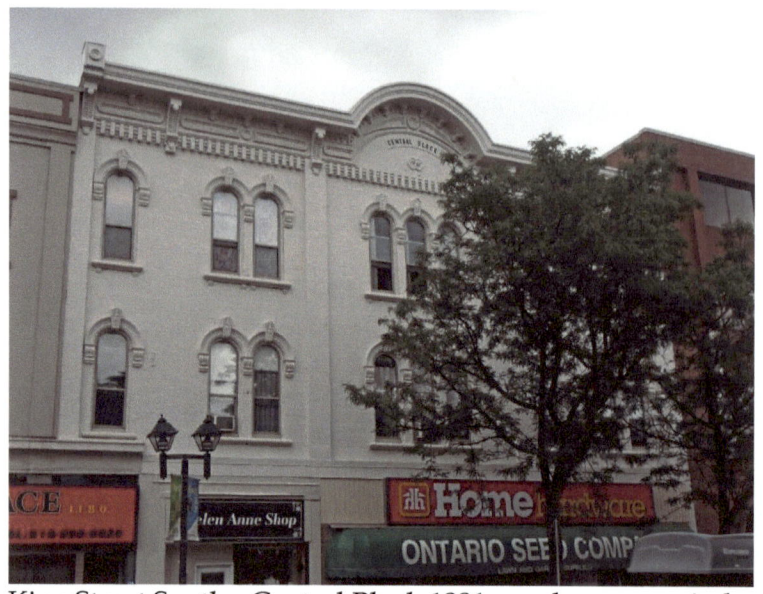

16 King Street South - Central Block 1881 – arches over windows, arched roofline, dentil moulding, and decorative cornice with brackets – Ontario Seed Company in operation since 1906

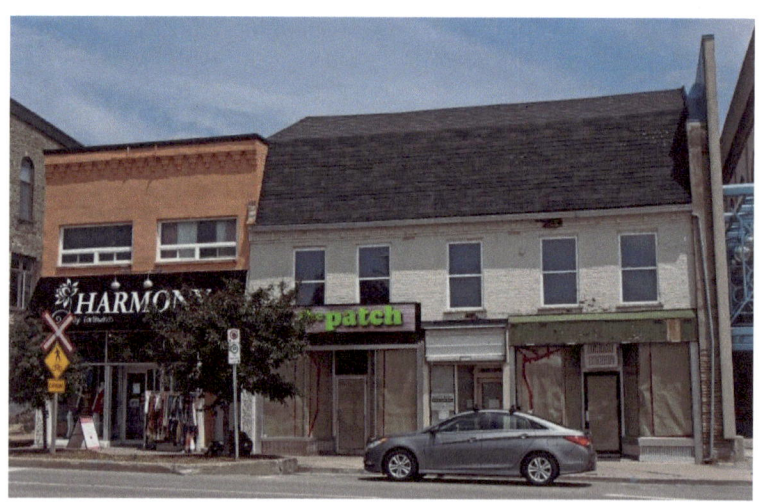

44-48 King Street South –Georgian, one of the oldest buildings in Waterloo built in 1849 – corbelled brickwork under the eaves

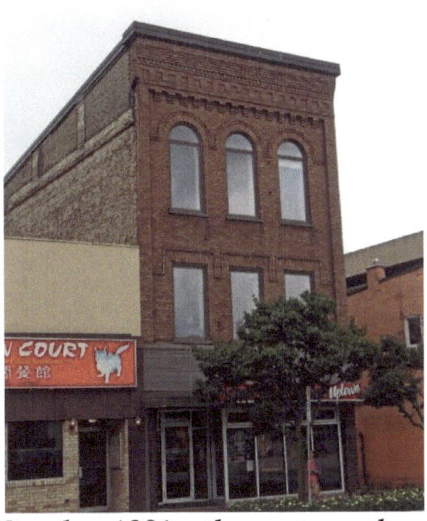

40 King Street South – 1901 – three-storey brown brick front, yellow brick rear - dentil moulding, arches over windows

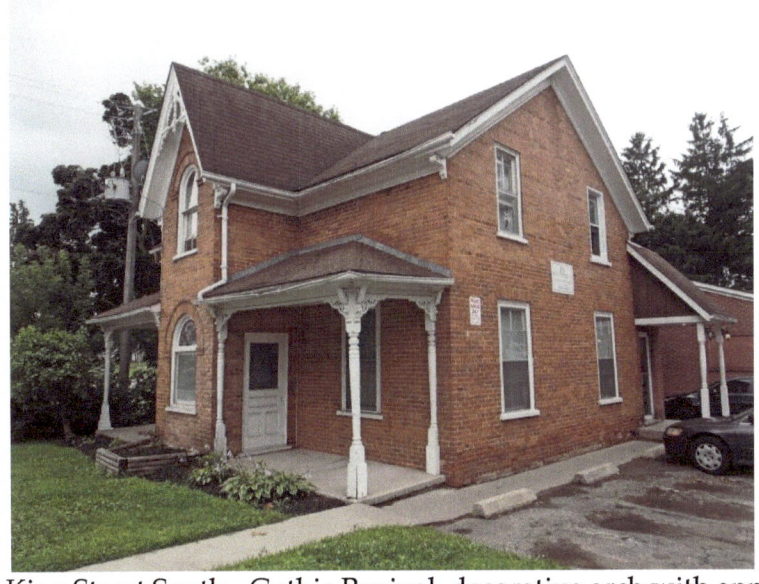

151 King Street South - Gothic Revival, decorative arch with applied scrollwork and spindles; turned verandah roof supports with delicate spindles

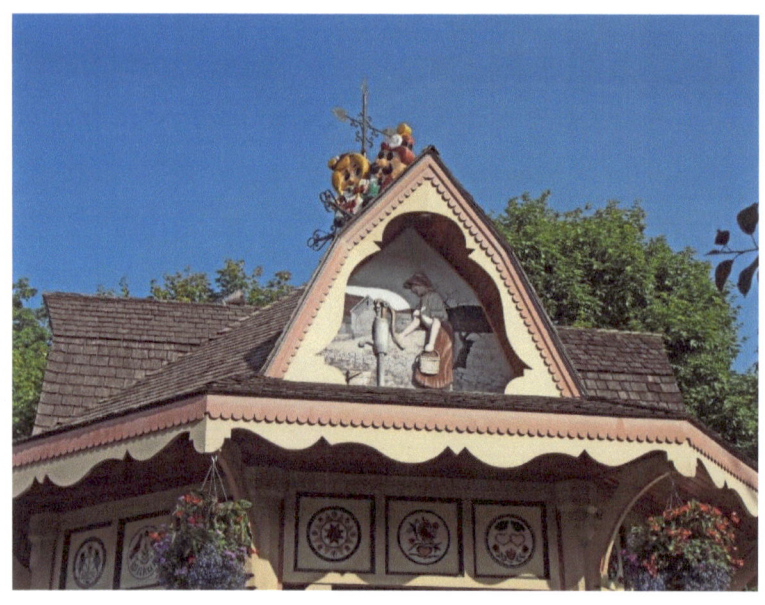

German/Austrian design of the gazebo in Brewmeister Green, Waterloo's oldest park with fountain and attractive floral displays

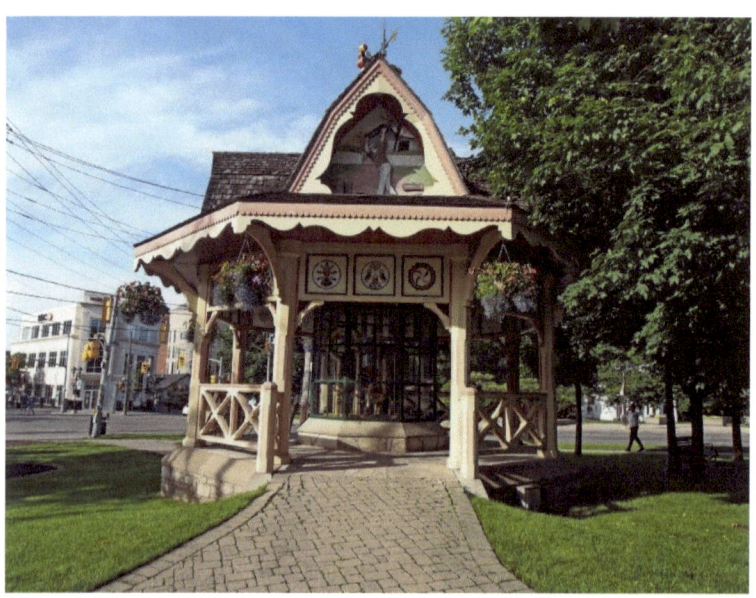

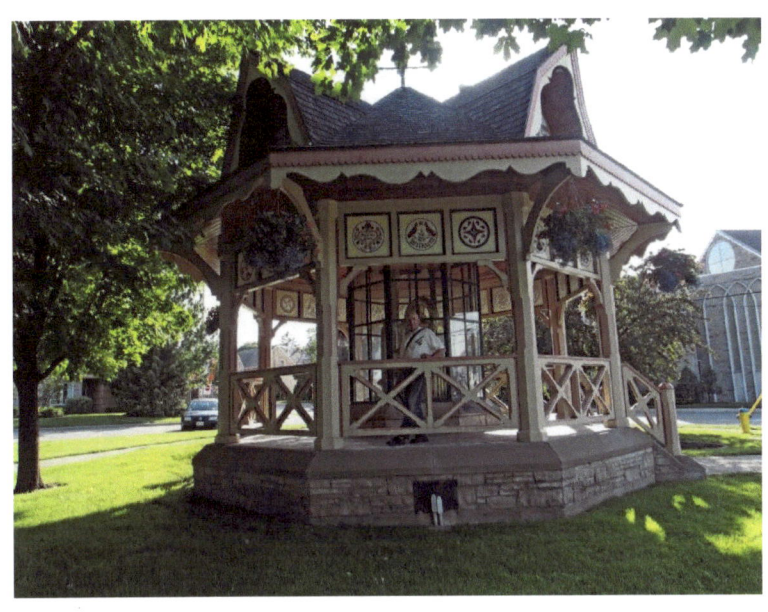

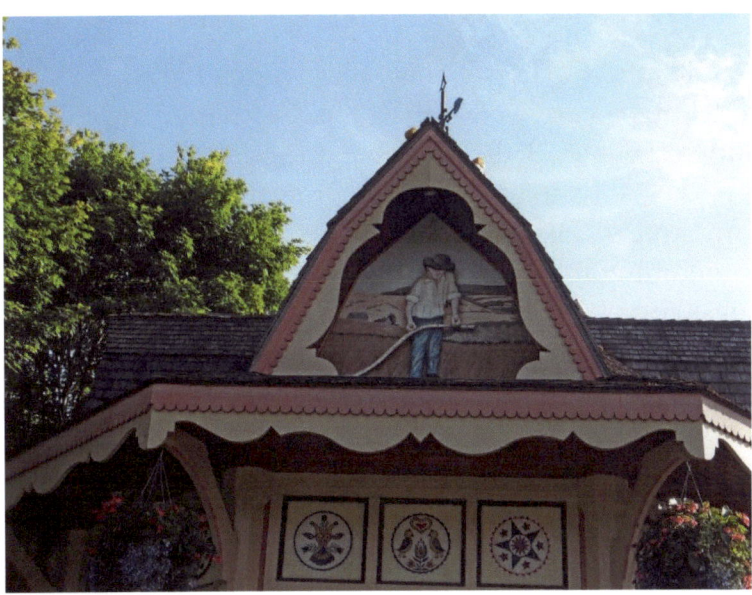

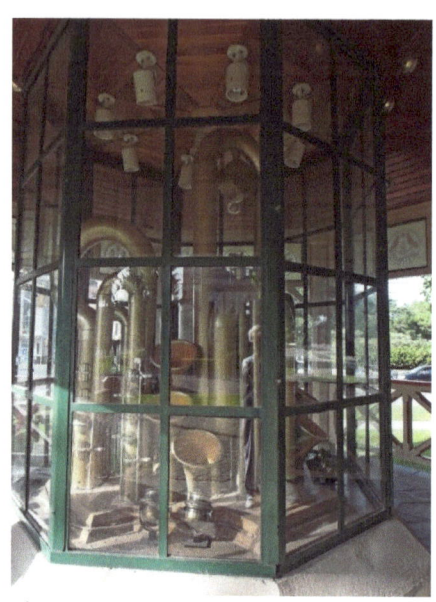

Oktoberfest Heritage Time Teller built in 1984

Kuntz/Carling/Labatt's Breweries 1860-1993
David Kuntz, a native of Weisbaden, Germany emigrated to
Canada in the late 1830s.  He moved to Waterloo in the mid-
1850s and established the "Spring Brewery" at King and
William Streets.  His son Louis took over management in the
1870s renaming it the "L. Kuntz Park Brewery".  It became the
Carling-Kuntz Brewery in 1929 with the name being
shortened to Carling Brewer in 1940.  Labatt Breweries of
Canada purchased the business in 1972.  It closed in 1992 and
the following year all the buildings were demolished.

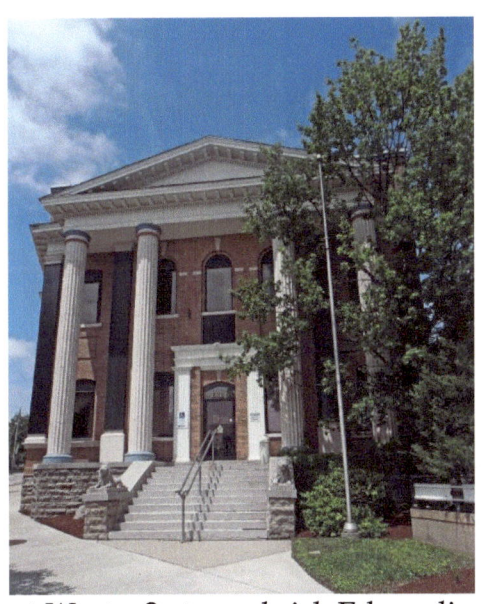

14 Erb Street West – 2-storey brick Edwardian building,
pediments, pilasters - the oldest part of the Waterloo Regional
Police Building was built in the 1880s – two storey columns,
1900 decorative figure lions gracing the front

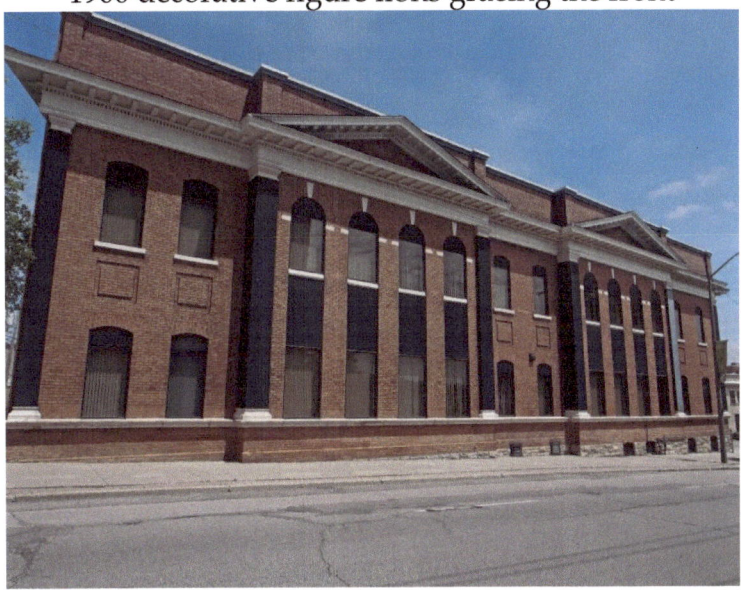

Later additions to the building

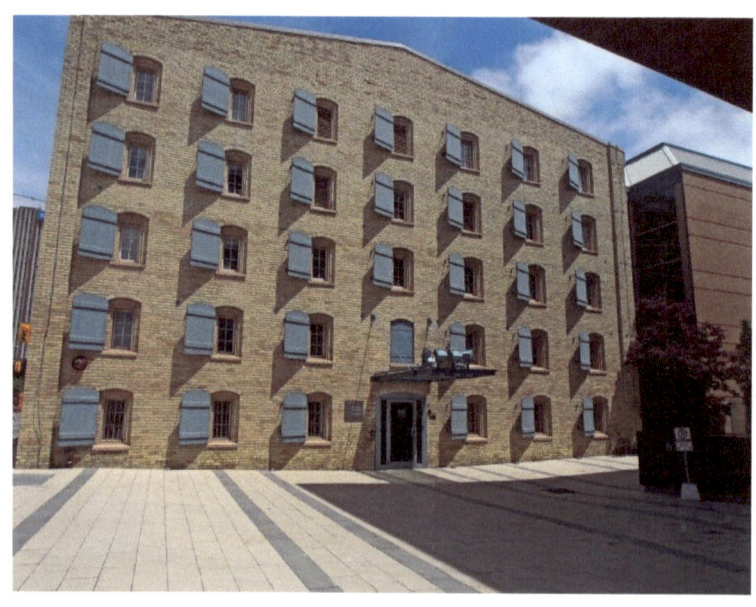

57 Erb Street West – former Seagram Bonded Warehouse built to store 6000 to 7000 oak barrels of whisky during the aging process – built in 1878; shallow sloped gable roof; brick pilasters on the corners of the building - now CIGI, Centre for International Governance Innovation

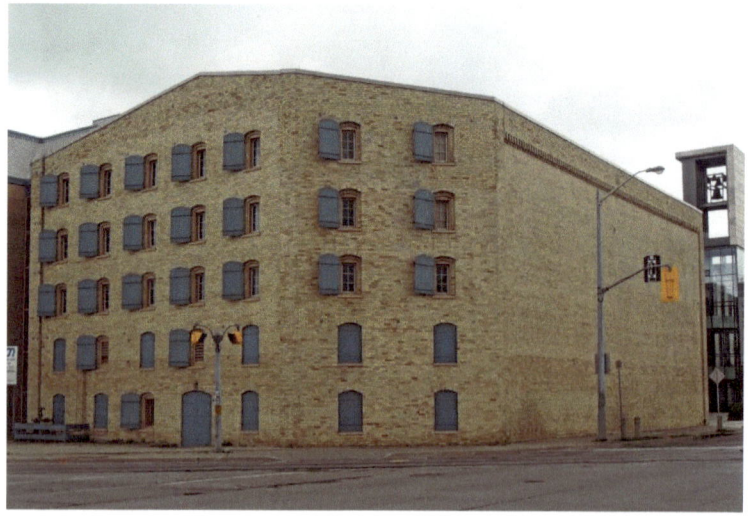

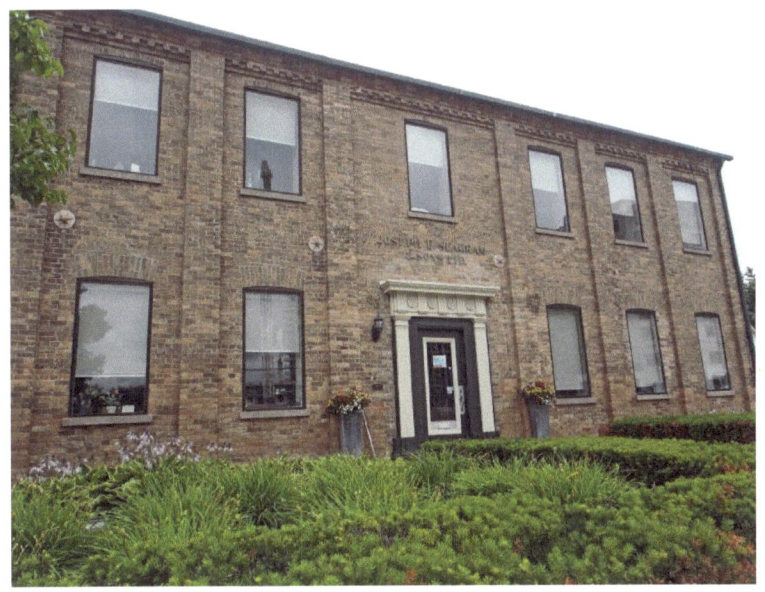

83 Erb Street West

Abraham Buehler's foundry at the corner of Erb and Euclid Streets shared the block on Erb with the granite Mills Distillery, at the corner of Caroline Street. The foundry was established in 1851. By 1864 Buehler had introduced steam power into his plant which produced a broad range of agricultural implements. In 1888 the firm merged with the Waterloo Foundry established by Jacob Bricker – the enlarged company, Waterloo Manufacturing Co., acquired a national reputation for heavy iron and steel engines, stoves, boilers and agricultural machinery. The business closed in 1890 and the property was sold to its neighbour to the east, the distillery which had been acquired in 1883 by Joseph E. Seagram.

Waterloo's core was at one time a buzzing hive of industry whose output, from flour to threshing machines, from shoes and gloves to cotton batts, beer and whiskey, was recognized and respected across the country.

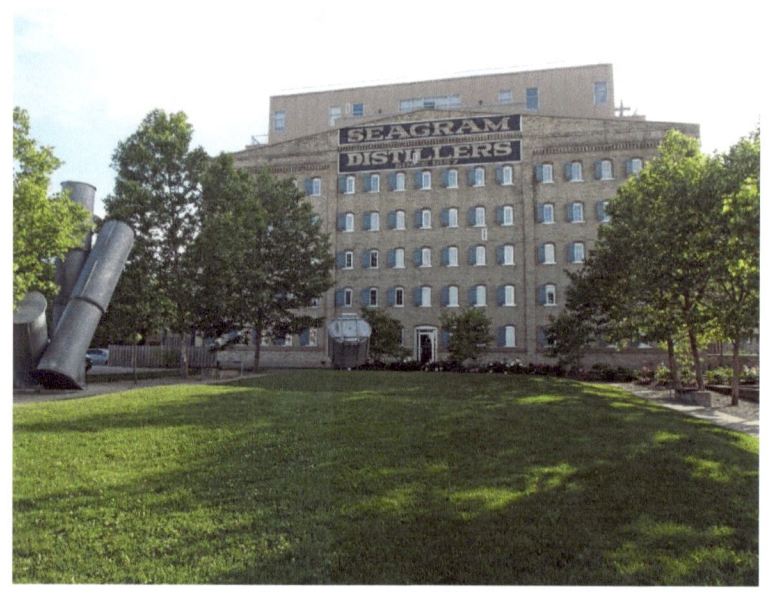

Seagram Distillers

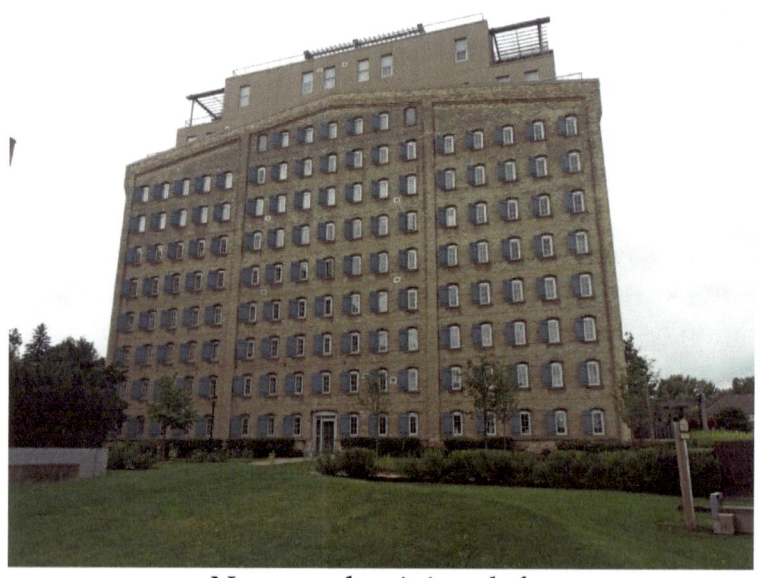

Now condominium lofts

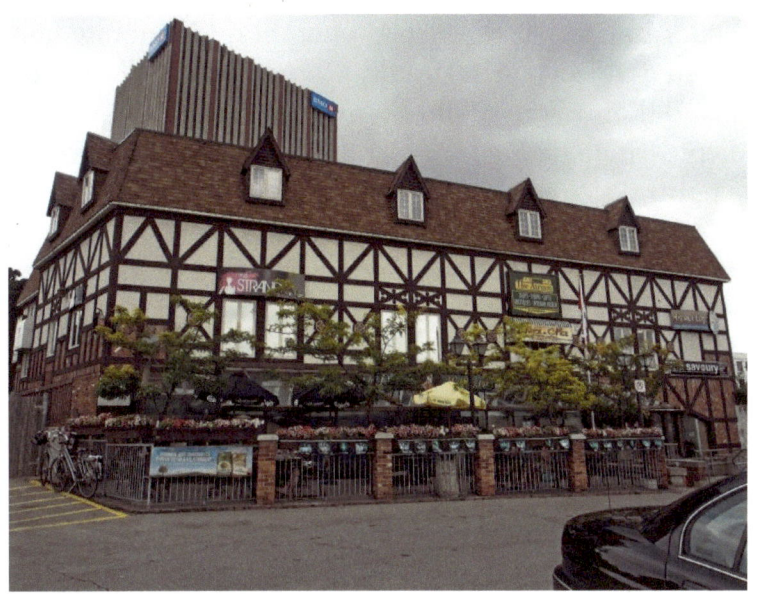

33 Erb Street West – Tudor style

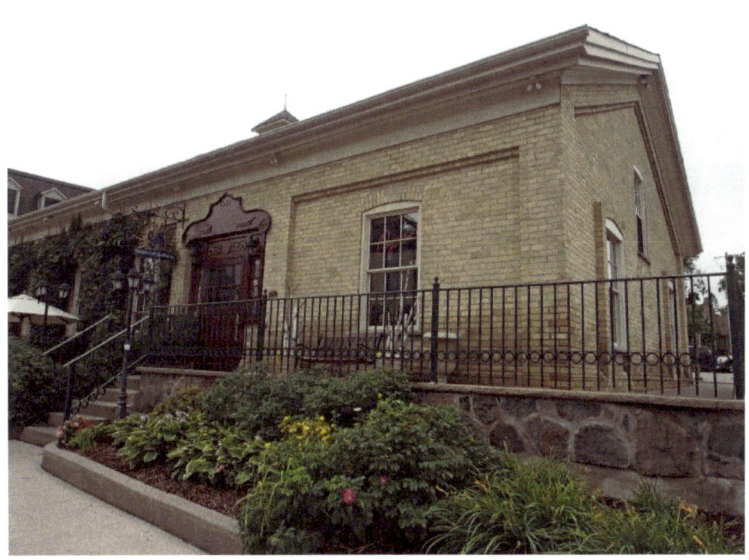

Erb Street West – established 1858

Martin Farmstead is a 6th generation Mennonite family farm located in RIM Park. David Martin, his wife Marie (nee Guth), and their twelve children migrated to this area in 1820. David constructed a log house and a barn on the property near a natural spring of water that continues to flow past the farmstead today. The architectural style is Mennonite-Georgian serving the Old Order Mennonite way of life with a kitchen garden, orchards, smoke house, drying house, and spring house.

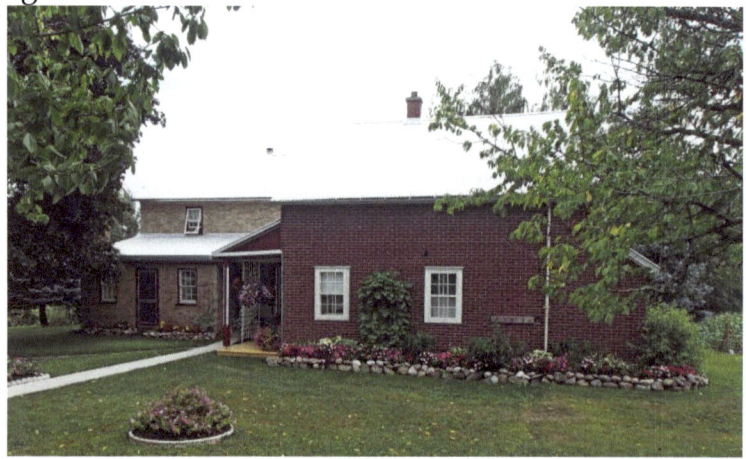

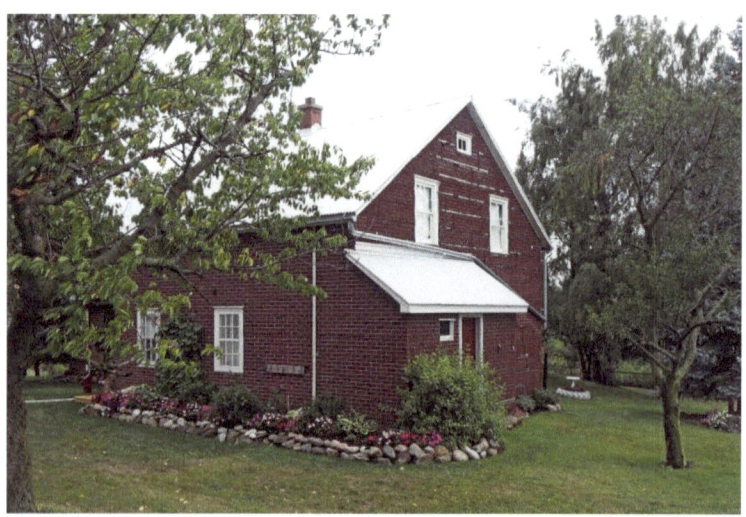

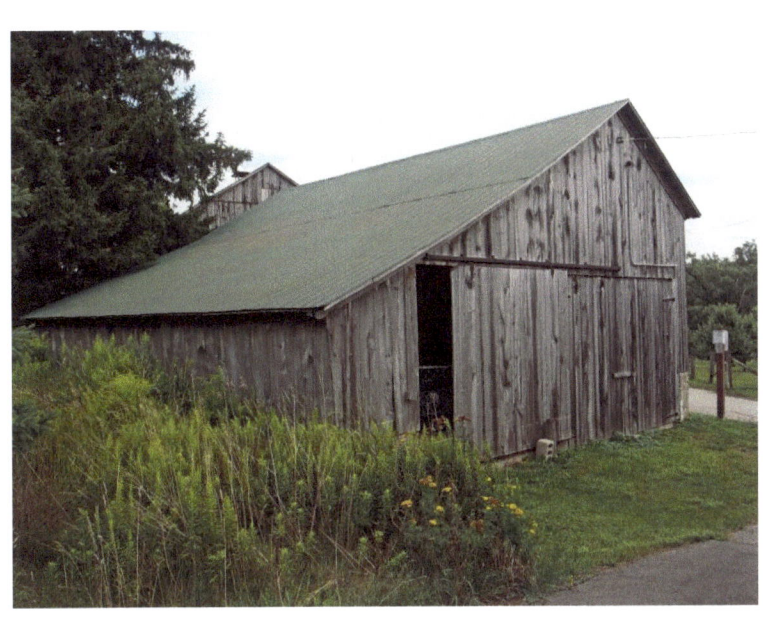

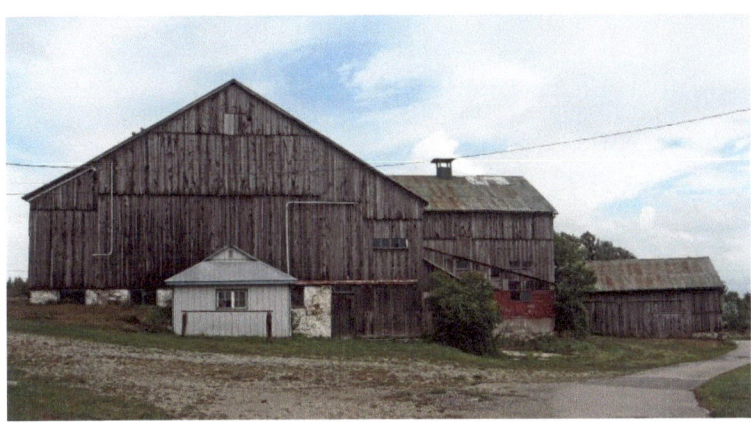

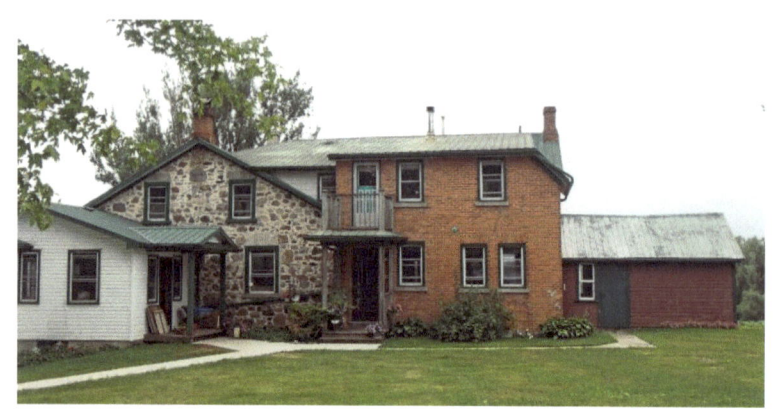

New Jerusalem Road

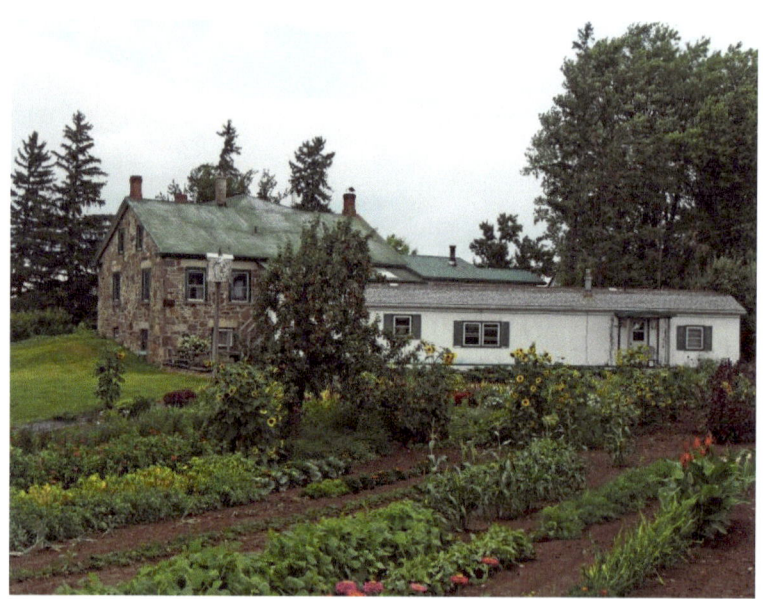

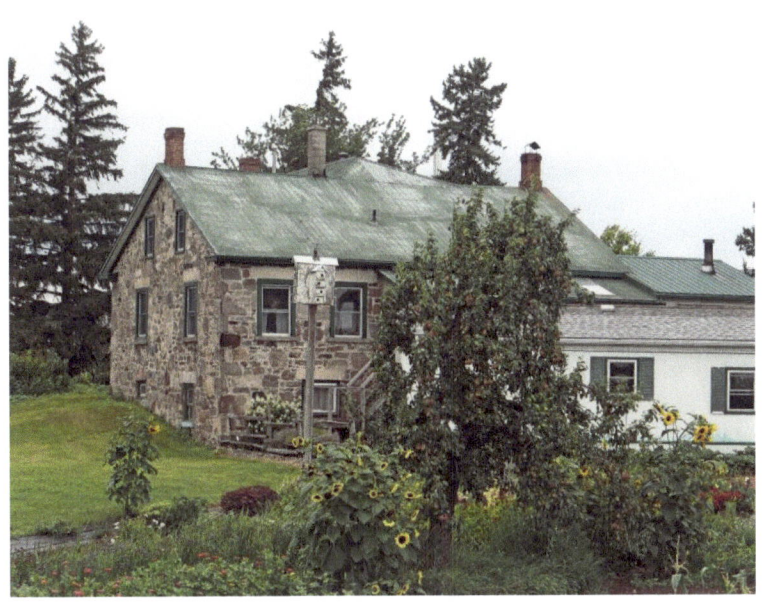

New Jerusalem Road

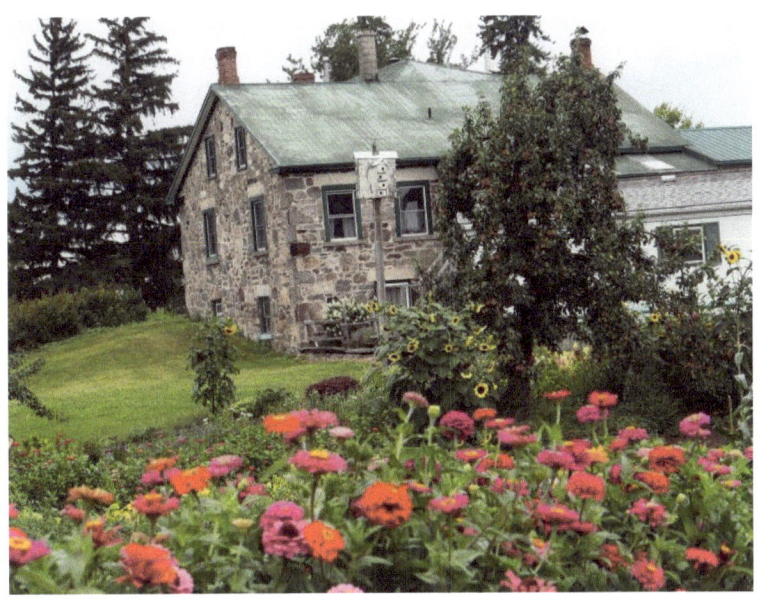

| | |
|---|---|
| **Bay Window:** A window that projects out from a wall, in a semicircular, rectangular, or polygonal design. Used frequently in Gothic and Victorian designs.<br><br>Example: 50 Albert Street, see Page 9 | |
| **Brackets**: a decorative or weight-bearing structural element which forms a right angle with one side against a wall and the other under a projecting surface such as an eave or roof.<br>Example: 85 Dorset Street, see Page 32 | |
| **Cobblestone (or rubble stone) architecture:** Refers to the use of cobblestones embedded in mortar as a method for erecting walls on houses and commercial buildings.<br>Example: 112 Albert Street, see Page 17 | |
| **Cornice**: originally the wooden overhang of the roof. With the use of stone, brick, iron and steel, the cornice is any horizontal moulded projection at the top of a building. They can be very decorative.<br>Example: 40 Albert Street, see Page 7 | |
| **Cornice Return:** decorative element on the end of a gable.<br>Example: 11 Central Street, see Page 30 | |
| **Course:** continuous horizontal row or layer of stone or brick.<br>Example: 4 King Street North, Page 39 | |

| | |
|---|---|
| **Dentil Moulding**: an even series of rectangles used as ornamental decoration in cornices.<br><br>Example: 40 King Street South, see Page 47 | |
| **Dormer**: (French for "sleep") a gable end window that pierces through the plane of a sloping roof surface to create usable space in the top floor or attic of a building by adding headroom.<br>Example: 35 King Street North, see Page 40 | |
| **Fretwork:** interlaced decorative design resembling a bracket<br><br>Example: 45 Young Street West, see Page 20 | |
| **Gable**: the triangular portion of a wall between the edges of a sloping roof.<br><br>Example: 36 Young Street West, see Page 19 | |
| **Gambrel Roof**: a symmetrical two-sided roof with two slopes on each side; the upper slope is positioned at a shallow angle, while the lower slope is steep.  It is similar to a mansard roof, a gambrel has vertical gable ends instead of being hipped at the four corners of the building.<br>Example: 29 Spring Street, see Page 27 | |

| | |
|---|---|
| **Iron Cresting**:  A decorative ornament along the top of a roof.  Iron cresting was popular in the Baroque era and also in Italianate, Victorian, Second Empire and Queen Anne styles of architecture. Example: 49-53 Albert St., Page 9 | 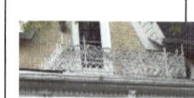 |
| **Keystones and Voussoirs**: a voussoir is a wedge-shaped element used in building an arch.  A keystone is the central stone that locks all the stones into position, allowing the arch to bear weight.  A keystone is often enlarged and embellished. Example: King Street North, Pg.42 |  |
| **Lintel:** horizontal part above a window or door that supports the structure above it. Example: 4 King Street North, Page 39 | 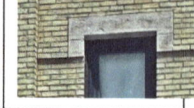 |
| **Palladian Window**: a large window that is divided into three sections with the centre section larger than the two side sections and usually arched. Example: 50 Albert Street, see Page 9 | 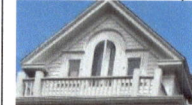 |
| **Parapet:** low wall around the edge of a roof.<br><br>Example: 4 King Street North, Page 39 | 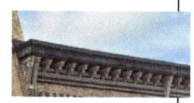 |
| **Pediment**: a triangular section above the door or portico, usually supported by columns.  The inside of the triangle is called the tympanum. Example: 40 Albert Street, see Page 7<br><br>Example: eared window pediments – 157 Albert Street, see Page 18 | 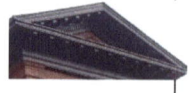<br>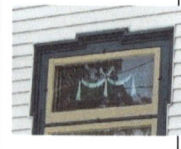 |

| | |
|---|---|
| **Pilaster**: a slightly projecting column built into or applied to the face of a wall for additional structural support.<br>Example: 40 Albert Street, see Page 7 | |
| **Sidelight**: a vertical window that flanks a door, and is often used to emphasize the importance of a primary entrance.<br>Example: 7 Central Street, see Page 31 | |
| **Transom Window:** the light above the doorway, also called a fanlight.<br><br>Example: 7 Central Street, see Page 31 | |
| **Turret:** a small tower that projects from the wall of a building.<br><br>Example: 84 Dorset Street, see Page 33 | |
| **Verge board and Finial**: also called bargeboards – hang from the projecting end of a roof and are often elaborately carved and ornamented. **Finial:** ornament added to the top of a gable, pinnacle, canopy or spire – a Gothic element.<br>Example: 7 Central Street, see Page 31 | |
| **Window Hood:** the piece found above window openings, usually of an ornate design, and covers the top third of the opening. Hoods are commonly placed above arched or curved openings on both windows and doors.<br>Example: 59 King Street North, see Page 38 | |

Building Styles

| | |
|---|---|
| Art Deco, 1910-1940 - The Art Deco Style was developed for the French luxury market after World War I. Art Deco left its mark on everything from lamps and foot stools to purses and hair combs. The style was adopted in Ontario by wealthy and very fashionable patrons who wanted Art Deco detailing to make their buildings look lavish and exotic. Example: 1 King Street North, see Page 44 | 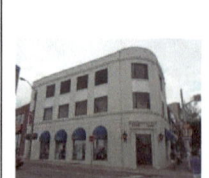 |
| Beaux Arts: Promoters of this style sought to express the classical principles on a grand and imposing scale.  Many of the Beaux Arts buildings were banks, post offices, and railway stations.  The Ontario Beaux Arts style is eclectic mixing elements of Classical, Renaissance and Baroque.  Often the designs have a temple-like façade, pedimented porticos, balustrades, capitals in many styles. Example: 3 King Street South, see Page 44 | 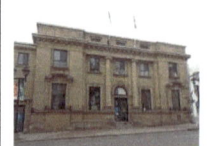 |
| Classical Revival (1820 - 1860) – This style was an analytical, scientific, and dogmatic revival based on intensive studies of Greek and Roman buildings, concerned with the application of Greek plans and proportions to civic buildings.  Schools, libraries, government offices, and most other civic buildings were built in the Classical Revival style. The white columned porches of the Classical Revival domestic buildings are identified with the mansions of wealthy land owners in Canada. Example: 40 Albert Street, see Page 7; and 27 King Street North, see Page 43 | 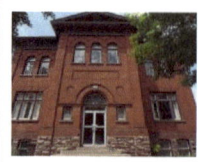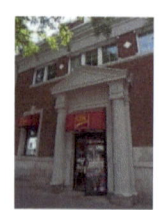 |

| | |
|---|---|
| Edwardian, 1900-1930 – This style bridges the ornate and elaborate styles of the Victorian era and the simplified styles of the 20th century. Balanced facades, simple roof lines, dormer windows, large front porches, and smooth brick surfaces are its characteristics.<br>Example: 50 Albert Street, see Page 9 | 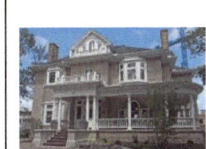 |
| Georgian, before 1860 – This style began with the British King Georges in the 18th century. These buildings have balanced facades around a central door, medium-pitched gable roofs, and small paned windows.<br>Example: 112 Albert Street, see Page 17 | 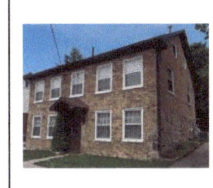 |
| Gothic Revival, 1830-1890 – These decorative buildings have sharply-pitched gables with highly detailed verge boards, pointed-arch window openings, and dichromatic brickwork. It is a common style in Ontario.<br>Example: 65 Albert Street, see Page 13 | 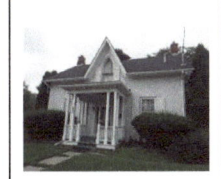 |
| Italianate, 1850-1900 – It has wide-bracketed eaves, belvederes, wrap-around verandahs.<br><br>Example: 101 Albert Street, see Page 16 | 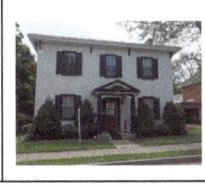 |

| | |
|---|---|
| Neo-Classical (1810 - 1850) – This style was a direct result of the War of 1812. Many Upper Canadians returning from the war with the United States were second or third generation Loyalists who had inherited land and means from their forefathers. Once the conflict had passed, they had the money and the time to expand their holdings and indulge their architectural whims. Both residential and commercial buildings were constructed on the traditional Georgian plan, but they had a new gaiety and light-heartedness. Detailing became more refined, delicate, and elegant.<br>Example: 95 Albert Street, see Page 15 | 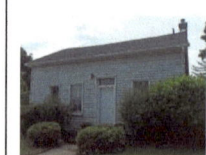 |
| Neocolonial (also Colonial Revival, Georgian Revival or Neo-Georgian) architecture seeks to revive elements of architectural style of American colonial architecture of the period around the Revolutionary War which drew strongly from Georgian architecture of Great Britain. Architecture from the 18th and early 19th centuries in Ontario includes a wide assortment of detailing and ornament applied to a design centered around the fireplace and the source of water. Structures are typically two stories, have a symmetrical front facade with elaborate front doorways, often with decorative crown pediments, fanlights, and sidelights, symmetrical windows flanking the front entrance, often in pairs or threes, and columned porches.<br>Example: 29 Spring Street, see Page 27 | 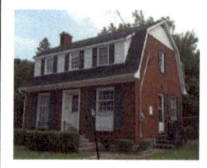 |

| | |
|---|---|
| Queen Anne, 1885-1900 – This style is distinguished by an irregular outline featuring a combination of an offset tower, broad gables, projecting two-storey bays, verandahs, multi-sloped roofs, and tall, decorative chimneys. A mixture of brick and wood is common. Windows often have one large single-paned bottom sash and small panes in the upper sash. Example: 79 Albert Street, see Page 14 | |
| Romanesque Revival, 1880-1910 – This style hearkens back to medieval architecture of the 11th and 12th centuries with a heavy appearance, blocky towers and rounded arches. Example: old Post Office, 35 King Street North, see Page 40 | |
| Tudor Revival - exposed timbers with stucco infill, multi-paned windows.<br><br>Example: 47 Albert Street, see Page 11 | |
| Vernacular/Traditional Mode 1638 - 1950 Influenced but not defined by a particular style, vernacular buildings are made from easily available materials and exhibit local design characteristics.<br>Example: 85 Dorset Street, see Page 32 | |
| Victorian - In Ontario, a Victorian style building can be seen as any building built between 1840 and 1900 that doesn't fit into any of the other categories. It encompasses a large group of buildings constructed in brick, stone, and timber, using an eclectic mixture of Classical and Gothic motifs.<br>Example: 54 Albert Street, see Page 12 | |

www.ingramcontent.com/pod-product-compliance
Lightning Source LLC
Chambersburg PA
CBHW040843180526
45159CB00001B/294